IN PHARAOH'S ARMY

Tobias Wolff's books include *Hunters in the Snow*, a collection of stories; *The Barracks Thief*, a short novel; *This Boy's Life*, a memoir; and he edited *The Picador Book of Contemporary American Stories*. His work has been translated widely and has received several awards, including the PEN/Faulkner Award and the Rea Award for the Short Story. Since 1980 he has been writer-in-residence at Syracuse University in upstate New York, where he lives with his wife Catherine and their three children.

Also by Tobias Wolff in Picador

The Stories of Tobias Wolff
which includes *Hunters in the Snow*,
In the Garden of the North American Martyrs,
and *The Barracks Thief*

This Boy's Life

The Picador Book of Contemporary American Stories (editor)

IN
PHARAOH'S
ARMY

Memories of a Lost War

TOBIAS WOLFF

PICADOR

First published in Great Britain 1994 by Bloomsbury Publishing plc

This edition published 1995 by Picador
an imprint of Macmillan Publishers Ltd
25 Eccleston Place, London SW1W 9NF
Basingstoke and Oxford
Associated companies throughout the world
www.macmillan.co.uk

ISBN 0 330 34019 0

Copyright © Tobias Wolff 1994

3 5 7 9 8 6 4 2

A CIP catalogue record for this book is available from
the British Library.

Printed and bound in Great Britain by
Mackays of Chatham plc, Chatham, Kent

For my brother, who gave me books

I would like to give special thanks again, and again, to my wife, Catherine, and to my editor, Gary Fisketjon, for their patient and thoughtful readings of this book. My gratitude as well to Amanda Urban, Geoffrey Wolff, and Michael Herr. Their help and friendship made all the difference.

You may well ask why I write. And yet my reasons are quite many. For it is not unusual in human beings who have witnessed the sack of a city or the falling to pieces of a people to desire to set down what they have witnessed for the benefit of unknown heirs or of generations infinitely remote; or, if you please, just to get the sight out of their heads.

– FORD MADOX FORD,
The Good Soldier

CONTENTS

PART ONE

Thanksgiving Special

Some peasants were blocking the road up ahead. I honked the horn but they chose not to hear. They were standing around under their pointed hats, watching a man and a woman yell at each other. When I got closer I saw two bicycles tangled up, a busted wicker basket, and vegetables all over the road. It looked like an accident.

Sergeant Benet reached over in front of me and sounded the horn again. It made a sheepish bleat, ridiculous coming from this armor-plated truck with its camouflage paint. The peasants turned their heads but they still didn't get out of the way. I was bearing down on them. Sergeant Benet slid low in the seat so nobody could get a look at him, which was prudent on his part, since he was probably the biggest man in this part of the province and certainly the only black man.

I kept honking the horn as I came on. The peasants held their ground longer than I thought they would, almost long enough to make me lose my nerve, then they jumped out of the way. I could hear them shouting and then I couldn't hear anything but the clang and grind of metal as the wheels of the truck passed over the bicycles. Awful sound. When I looked in the rearview most of the peasants were staring after the truck while a few others inspected the wreckage in the road.

Sergeant Benet sat up again. He said, without reproach, "That's a shame, sir. That's just a real shame."

I didn't say anything. What could I say? I hadn't done it for fun. Seven months back, at the beginning of my tour, when I was still calling them people instead of peasants, I wouldn't have run over their bikes. I would have slowed down or even stopped until they decided to move their argument to the side of the road, if it was a real argument and not a setup. But I didn't stop anymore. Neither did Sergeant Benet. Nobody did, as these peasants – these people – should have known.

We passed through a string of hamlets without further interruption. I drove fast to get an edge on the snipers, but snipers weren't the problem on this road. Mines were the problem. If I ran over a touch-fused 105 shell it wouldn't make any difference how fast I was going. I'd seen a two-and-a-half-ton truck blown right off the road by one of those, just a few vehicles ahead of me in a convoy coming back from Saigon. The truck jumped like a bucking horse and landed on its side in the ditch. The rest of us stopped and hit the dirt, waiting for an ambush that never came. When we finally got up and looked in the truck there was nobody there, nothing you could think of as a person. The two Vietnamese soldiers inside had been turned to chowder by the blast coming up through the floor of the cab. After that I always packed sandbags under my seat and on the floorboards of anything I drove. I suspected that even the scant comfort I took from these doleful measures was illusory, but illusions kept me going and I declined

4

to pursue any line of thought that might put them in danger.

We were all living on fantasies. There was some variation among them, but every one of us believed, instinctively if not consciously, that he could help his chances by observing certain rites and protocols. Some of these were obvious. You kept your weapon clean. You paid attention. You didn't take risks unless you had to. But that got you only so far. Despite the promise implicit in our training – *If you do everything right, you'll make it home* – you couldn't help but notice that the good troops were getting killed right along with the slackers and shitbirds. It was clear that survival wasn't only a function of Zero Defects and Combat Readiness. There had to be something else to it, something unreachable by practical means.

Why one man died and another lived was, in the end, a mystery, and we who lived paid court to that mystery in every way we could think of. I carried a heavy gold pocket watch given to me by my fiancée. It had belonged to her grandfather, and to her father. She'd had it engraved with a verse from Kahlil Gibran's *The Prophet*. It went with me everywhere, rain or shine. That it continued to tick I regarded as an affirmation somehow linked to my own continuance, and when it got stolen toward the end of my tour I suffered through several days of stupefying fatalism.

The ordinary human sensation of occupying a safe place in a coherent scheme allowed me to perform, to help myself as much as I could. But at times I was seized and shaken by the certainty that nothing I did meant anything, and all around me I sensed currents of hatred and malign intent. When I felt it coming on I gave a sudden wrenching shudder as if I'd bitten into something sour, and forced my thoughts elsewhere. To consider the reality of my situation only made it worse.

Not that my situation was all that bad, compared to what it might have been. I was stationed in the Delta at a time when things were much quieter there than up north. Up north they were fighting big North Vietnamese Army units. Tens of thousands of men had died for places that didn't even have names, just elevation numbers or terms of utility – Firebase Zulu, Landing Zone Oscar – and which were usually evacuated a few days after the battle, when the cameras had gone back to Saigon. The NVA were very hard cases. They didn't hit and run like the Vietcong; they hit and kept hitting. I kept hearing things: that they had not only mortars but heavy artillery, lugged down mountain trails piece by piece as in the days of Dienbienphu; that before battle they got stoned on some kind of special communist reefer that made them suicidally brave; that their tunnels were like cities and ran right under our bases; that they had tanks and helicopters; that American deserters were fighting on their side.

These were only a few of the rumors. I doubted them, but of course some question always remained, and every so often one would prove to be true. Their tunnels did run under our bases. And later, at Lang Vei, they did use tanks against us. The idea of those people coming at us with even a fraction of the hardware we routinely turned on them seemed outrageous, an atrocity.

The Delta was different. Here the enemy were local guerrillas organized in tight, village-based cadres. Occasionally they combined for an attack on one of our compounds or to ambush a convoy of trucks or boats, or even a large unit isolated in the field and grown sloppy from long periods without contact, but most of the time they worked in small teams and stayed out of sight. They blew us up with homemade mines fashioned from dud howitzer shells, or real American mines bought from our South Vietnamese allies. They dropped mortars on us at night – never very many; just enough, with luck, to kill a man or two, or inflict some wounds, or at least scare us half to death. Then they hightailed it home before our fire-direction people could vector in on them, slipped into bed, and, as I imagined, laughed themselves to sleep. They booby-trapped our trucks and jeeps. They booby-trapped the trails they knew we'd take, because we always took the same trails, the ones that looked easy and kept us dry. They sniped at us. And every so often, when they felt called on to prove that they were sincere guerrillas and not just farmers acting tough, they crowded a road with animals or children and shot the sentimentalists who stopped.

We did not die by the hundreds in pitched battles. We died a man at a time, at a pace almost casual. You could sometimes begin to feel safe, and then you caught yourself and looked around, and you saw that of the people you'd known at the beginning of your tour a number were dead or in hospitals. And you did some nervous arithmetic. In my case the odds were not an actuary's dream, but they could have been worse. A lot worse, in fact. Terrible, in fact.

Back in the States I'd belonged to the Special Forces, first as an enlisted man and then as an officer. As part of my training I'd spent a year studying Vietnamese and learned to speak the language like a seven-year-old child with a freakish military vocabulary. This facility of mine, recorded in my file, caught the eye of a personnel officer during my first couple of hours in Vietnam, as I was passing through the reception center at Bien Hoa. He told me that a Vietnamese artillery battalion outside My Tho was in need of an adviser with a command of the language. Later on, when a replacement was available, I could request a transfer back into the Special Forces. He apologized for the assignment. He figured I'd been itching for some action, more than I was likely to get in the Delta, and was sorry to disappoint me.

I saw it as a reprieve. Several men I'd gone through training with had been killed or wounded in recent months, overrun in their isolated outposts, swallowed up while on patrol, betrayed by the mercenary troops they led. My best friend in the army, Hugh Pierce, had been killed a few months before I shipped out, and this gave me a shock I've never really gotten over. In those days I was scared stiff. The feeling was hardly unique over there, but I did have good reason for it: I was completely incompetent to lead a Special Forces team. This was adamant fact, not failure of nerve. My failure of nerve took another form. I wanted out, but I lacked the courage to confess my incompetence as the price of getting out. I was ready to be killed, even, perhaps, get others killed, to avoid that humiliation.

So this personnel officer gave me a way out: if not with honor, at least with the appearance of it. But later that day, drinking in the bar at the receiving center, I changed my mind. After all, it was honor itself that I wanted, true honor, not some passable counterfeit but the kind you could live on the rest of your life. I would refuse the Delta post. I would demand to be sent to the Special Forces, to wherever the latest disaster had created an opening, and hope that by some miracle I'd prove a better soldier than I knew myself to be.

I strengthened my resolve with gin and tonic all through the afternoon. In early evening I left the bar and made my way back to the transients' barracks. It was hot. A few steps out of the air-conditioning and I was faint, wilting, my uniform plastered to my skin. Near my quarters a party of newly arrived enlisted men sat outside one of the in-processing barns, smoking, silent, trying to look like killers. They didn't. Their greenness was apparent at a glance, as mine must have been. They still had flesh on their cheeks. Their uniforms hung light on them, without the greasy sag of a thousand sweat baths. And their eyes were still lively and curious. But even if I hadn't noticed these things I would have recognized them as new guys by their look of tense, offended isolation. It came as a surprise to men joining this hard enterprise that instead of being welcomed they were shunned. But that's what happened. You noticed it as soon as you got off the plane.

That night we had an alert. I found out later it was just a probe on the perimeter, but I didn't know this while it was going on and neither did anyone else. The airfield had already been hit by sappers. People had been killed, several planes and helicopters blown up. It could happen again. You know that an attack is "just a probe" only after it's over. I stood outside with other fresh arrivals and watched bellowing, half-dressed men run by in different directions. Trucks raced past, some with spinning lights like police cruisers. Between the high, excited bursts of M-16 fire

I could hear heavy machine guns pounding away, deep and methodical. Flares popped overhead. They covered everything in a cold, quivering light.

No one came to tell us what was going on. We hadn't received our issue of combat gear, so we had no weapons or ammunition, no flak jackets, not even a steel helmet. We were helpless. And nobody knew or cared. They had forgotten about us – more to the point, forgotten about me. In this whole place not one person was thinking of me, thinking, Christ, I better take a run over there and see how Lieutenant Wolff is doing! No. I wasn't on anybody's mind. And I understood that this was true not only here but in every square inch of this country. Not one person out there cared whether I lived or died. Maybe some tender hearts cared in the abstract, but it was my fate to be a particular person, and about me as a particular person there was an undeniable, comprehensive lack of concern.

It isn't true that not one person cared. I cared. It seemed to me I cared too much, cared more than was manly or decent. I could feel my life almost as a thing apart, begging me for protection. It was embarrassing. Truly, my fear shamed me. In the morning I went back to the personnel officer and asked him to change my orders. He told me it was too late, but promised he would note my wish to be transferred to the Special Forces. Later that day I boarded a helicopter for the Delta.

The Vietnamese division to which my battalion belonged was headquartered in My Tho, on the Mekong River. My Tho was an old province capital. The streets were wide and lined with trees. A reservoir ran through a park in the middle of town. The houses had red tile roofs, flowerpots on their windowsills and doorsteps. There were crumbling stucco mansions along the boulevard that fronted the river, their walls still bearing traces of the turquoise, salmon, and lavender washes ordered from France by their previous owners. Most had been turned into apartment houses, a few others into hotels. They had tall shuttered windows and wrought-iron balconies overlooking the street. As you walked past the open doorways you felt a cool breath from the courtyards within, heard the singing of birds, the trickle of water in stone fountains. Across the street, on the bank of the river, was a line of restaurants and bars and antique stores, also a watch repair shop famous in its own right for stealing the movements from Omegas and Rolexes and replacing them with movements of more neighborly manufacture. You could always recognize a fellow from My Tho by the wildly spinning hands on his Oyster Perpetual.

I'd never been to Europe, but in My Tho I could almost imagine myself there. And that was the whole point. The French had made the town like this so they could imagine themselves in France. The illusion was just about perfect, except for all the Vietnamese.

It was a quiet, dreamy town, and a lucky town. For a couple of years now there'd been no car bombs, no bombs in restaurants, no kidnappings, no assassinations. Not in the city limits, anyway. That was very unusual, maybe even unique among province capitals in Vietnam. It didn't seem possible that luck alone could explain it; there had to be a reason. One theory you heard was that the province chief had been paying tribute to the local Vietcong: not only dollars stolen from the American aid program but American arms and medicine, which he then reported as lost to enemy activity. It was also said that My Tho was an R and R spot for exhausted and wounded guerrillas, their own little Hawaii, and that over time an arrangement had evolved: Don't bother us and we won't bother you. Either of these explanations might have been true, or both, but there was definitely some kind of agreement in effect. The town had a druidical circle around it. Inside, take it easy. Outside, watch your ass. My battalion was outside the circle, and I could feel the unseen but absolute gate slam shut behind me every time I left.

My Tho was lucky in another way. Almost no Americans were allowed in town, only a few AID people and those of us who were assigned to the Vietnamese military. By some stratagem My Tho had managed to get itself declared off-limits to regular American troops, and that was its deliverance, because there were several thousand of them up the road at Dong Tam just dying to come in and trash the place.

I was glad the American troops were kept out. Without even meaning to they would have turned the people into prostitutes, pimps, pedicab drivers, and thieves, and the town itself into a nest of burger stands and laundries. Within months it would have been unrecognizable; such was the power of American dollars and American appetites. Besides, I didn't want my stock watered down. I took pleasure in being one of a very few white men among all these dark folk, big among the small, rich among the poor. My special position did not make me arrogant, not at first. It made me feel benevolent, generous, protective, as if I were surrounded by children, as I often was – crowds of them, shy but curious, taking turns stroking my hairy arms and, as a special treat, my mustache. In My Tho I had a sense of myself as father, even as lord, the very sensation that, even more than all their holdings here, must have made the thought of losing this place unbearable to the French.

So the American grunts had to keep to their base in Dong Tam, but even in that miserable shithole they had some advantages over those of us who lived with the Vietnamese. They were more secure, as long as they stayed inside the wire. Outside the wire was another story. But inside they were fairly safe, protected by their numbers and by a vast circle of minefields, heavily manned bunkers with interlocking fields of fire, tanks, mobile artillery, and any kind of air support they wanted, in any quantity, at any hour of the day or night. The situation at my battalion was very different. We were stuck by ourselves – one hundred fifty or so men and six howitzers – in a field surrounded by rice paddies. A canal ran along one leg of our perimeter. The water was deep, the muddy banks sheer and slick; it would be hard to attack us from that side. But the canal was the only help we got from topography. Otherwise the land around us was flat and open and laced with dikes, enough of them to move an army over while another army marched up the road to our front gate. It was a terrible site, chosen for reasons incomprehensible to me.

The troops at Dong Tam were better protected than we were, and better supplied. We were expected to live like our Vietnamese counterparts, which sounded like a noble project, democratic, right-minded, the perfect show of partnership with our hosts and allies – a terrific idea, really, until you actually tried it. Not many did, only a few advisers in the way outback who went the whole nine yards, sleeping in hammocks, eating rats, and padding around on rubber sandals that they swore up and down were better than boots. I admired them, but my own intention was to live not as a Vietnamese among Vietnamese but as an American among Vietnamese.

Living like an American wasn't easy. Outside the big bases it was a full-time job. When Sergeant Benet and I first arrived at the battalion, the advisers we were supposed to replace were living very close to the bone, or so it seemed to us. They ate C rations. They slept in sleeping bags, on field cots. For light they used oil lamps borrowed from the Vietnamese quartermaster. Sergeant Benet and I agreed that we owed ourselves something better.

We started to scrounge. There wasn't much else to do. We were advisers, but we didn't know exactly what advice we were supposed to be giving, or to whom. We rarely saw Major Chau, the battalion commander, and when we did he seemed embarrassed, at a loss as to why we were there. At first he seemed suspicious of us. Maybe he thought we were supposed to be keeping tabs on him. He had good reason to fear scrutiny, but then so did every officer of rank in that unhappy army. All of them were political intriguers; they had to be in order to receive promotion and command. Their wages were too low to live on because it was assumed they'd be stealing, so they stole. They were punished for losing men in battle, therefore they avoided battle. When their men deserted they kept them on the roster and continued to draw their pay, with the result that the losses were never made up and the units turned into

14

scarecrow remnants hardly able to defend themselves, let alone carry the war to the enemy. Our own battalion was seriously understrength.

I was a pretty good scrounge. Not of the same champion breed as Sergeant Benet, but pretty good. We became partners in horse trading. I was lonely and callow enough to have let friendship happen too, even across the forbidden distance of our ranks, but he knew better and protected me from myself. He never forgot that I was an officer. Even in anger, and I sometimes brought him to anger, he called me sir. This was partly out of habit, the old soldier respectful always of the commission if not the uncertain, hopelessly compromised man who held it. But it was also his way of staying out of reach so he could have a life apart. Still, I could make him laugh, and I knew that he liked me, probably more than he wanted to.

We couldn't mooch off the Vietnamese, because they didn't have anything. We had to do our business with the Americans at Dong Tam. At first we simply begged, presenting ourselves as orphans at the gate, hungry, unsheltered, defenseless. This didn't get us very far. As more than one supply sergeant said, they weren't running a charity. If we wanted to play we had to bring something to the party. What we ended up bringing were souvenirs. Most of the men at Dong Tam were support troops who rarely left the base. They never saw any action, nor for that matter did most of the soldiers who did go into the field. The letters they wrote home didn't always make this clear. In their boredom they sometimes allowed themselves to say things that weren't strictly true, and in time, as they approached the end of their tours, a fever came upon them to find some enemy artifacts to back up the stories they'd been telling their friends and girlfriends and little brothers.

This stuff was easy enough for us to come by. Sergeant Benet mentioned our needs to some of the battalion officers, and for a consideration in the form of Courvoisier, Marlboros, Seiko watches, and other such goods, cheap in the PX and dear on the street, they set up a pipeline for us: Vietcong flags and battle standards, all convincingly worn and shredded, with unit designations and inspiring communist slogans in Vietnamese; bloodstained VC identity cards; brass belt buckles embossed with hammer and sickle; bayonets similarly decorated; pith helmets of the kind worn by the enemy; and Chicom rifles. Major Chau himself never demanded anything in so many words, and he always accepted what we gave him with a gracious show of surprise. He seemed relieved to find us willing to forgo the steel-jawed American rectitude practiced on him by our predecessors and get down to the business of business. This wasn't just cynicism and greed. One of our transactions at Dong Tam netted us a haul of claymore mines, each packing hundreds of ball bearings. If we got attacked they would help fill the holes left by our missing men. We also brought home sandbags, cement, and barbed wire to beef up our perimeter, beehive rounds for the howitzers, and more mines – you could never have too many mines. Fifty thousand wouldn't have been too many for me. Given the chance, I'd have lived smack in the middle of a minefield twenty miles wide. Anyway, in Major Chau's situation, which was now our situation, making deals was how you got by.

Chicom rifles were our most valuable stock-in-trade. The other stuff could be faked, and probably was. Why not?

What can be faked will be faked. If the locals could put together movements for watches, even ones that ran funny, they wouldn't have any trouble turning out Vietcong flags and identity cards. In fact some of them must have been producing these things for the VC all along, which put the whole question of authenticity in a new light: if made by the same hands, would enemy equipment be any less real because it was ordered by us instead of them?

We never accused our suppliers of dealing in counterfeits, nor did our agents at Dong Tam accuse us. But they employed a certain tilt of the head when handling fakable items, and allowed their pursed lips the faintest quiver of suppressed mirth. They took what we offered, but at a discount. Only the Chicoms commanded their respect.

The Chicom was a heavy, bolt-action rifle with a long bayonet that folded down along the barrel when not in use. It was manufactured in communist China – hence its nickname. Vietminh soldiers had carried it against the French, and the Vietcong had carried it against us when this war began. They didn't use it much anymore, not when they could get their hands on AK-47s or M-16s, but the Chicom was a very mean-looking weapon, and indisputably a communist weapon. The perfect trophy. Some of the guys at Dong Tam even had them chromed, like baby shoes and the engine blocks of their cars.

By the end of the year Sergeant Benet and I were living in a wooden hooch with screens on the windows. We had bunks with mattresses. We had electric lights, a TV, a stereo, a stove, a refrigerator, and a generator to keep it all running. But the TV was a black-and-white portable. It was okay for the news, but we really felt the pinch when *Bonanza* came on. We were *Bonanza* freaks, Sergeant Benet and I. They were broadcasting a two-hour *Bonanza* special on Thanksgiving night, and we meant to watch this properly, on a color TV with a big screen. Sergeant Benet had arranged a deal that would significantly upgrade our viewing pleasure, a Chicom for a 21-inch set. Everything was set. That was why he and I were on the road to Dong Tam the day I ran over the bikes, Thanksgiving Day, 1967.

I drove fast. We'd started late, after trying all morning to find a convoy we could attach ourselves to. There weren't any. Driving there alone would be dangerous, stupid, we both knew that, and we agreed to call the trip off until we had some other people around us, some padding, but I couldn't get my mind off that Thanksgiving special. I fooled around with paperwork for a couple of hours after lunch, then gave up and said the hell with it, I was going.

Sergeant Benet said he'd go too, and though I could see he didn't like the idea I made no effort to talk him out of it.

He held hard to the handle on the dash while I slithered in the ruts and splashed through muddy holes and found impossible paths between the people on the road. As I drove I indulged a morbid habit I couldn't seem to break, picking places in the distance ahead and thinking, There – that's where I'm going to get it . . . seeing the mine erupt through the mud, through the floorboard, the whole picture going red. Then I was on the place and past the place, and everything that was clenched and cowering opened in a rush. A few minutes later, not even thinking about it, or pretending not to think about it, I chose another place and thought, There –

Sergeant Benet fiddled with the radio, which wasn't working right. No radio in Vietnam ever worked right.

The VC had blown the bridge a few months back, so we had to take the old ferry across the river. Then up past another hamlet, and another, and the blackened ruins of a militia outpost, and on, and on.

How far was it to Dong Tam? Hard to say, all these years later. But it would have been hard to say then too, because distance had become a psychological condition rather than a measurable issue of meters and kilometers. A journey down these roads was endless until you arrived at the end. No "seems" about it: it was endless until it was over. That was the truth of distance. The same with time. Our tour of duty was a year, but neither I nor anyone else ever used the word. You never heard it at all. The most we dared speak of were days, and even a day could lose you in its vast expanse, its limits stretching outward beyond the grasp of imagination.

Indeed, just about everything in our world had become relative, subjective. We were lied to, and knew it. Misinformed, innocently and by design. Confused. We couldn't trust our own intelligence, in any sense of that word. Rumors festered in our uncertainty. Rumors, lies, apprehension, distant report, wishful thinking, such were the lenses through which we regarded this *terra infirma* and its maddeningly self-possessed, ungrateful people, whom we necessarily feared and therefore hated and could never understand. Where were we, really? Who was who, what was what? The truth was not forthcoming, you had to put it together for yourself, and in this way your most fantastic nightmares and suspicions became as real to you as the sometimes unbelievable fact of being in this place at all. Your version of reality might not tally with the stats or the map or the after-action report, but it was the reality you lived in, that would live on in you through the years ahead, and become the story by which you remembered all that you had seen, and done, and been.

So, once again, how far was it to Dong Tam? Far enough. And how long did it take? Forever, until you got there.

We turned a corner and were on the final approach. The road was lined with beer shanties and black market stands. Red-mouthed girls in fishnet stockings and miniskirts squawked from the doorways, wobbling on high heels. Out beyond the line of hovels I could see farmers in watery fields, some astride buffalo, most on foot, bent down like cranes, pant legs gathered above their knees, working right up to the edge of the minefield.

Sergeant Benet unloaded our rifles as we pulled up to the gate. The sentries usually waved us through when they saw we were American, but this time we got stopped. A big MP captain came out of the guard shack and stuck his head inside the window. He was one of those pink-skinned people who disintegrate in daylight. His nose was peeling, his lips were blistered, his eyes bloodshot. Without due ceremony, he asked me what our business was.

I said, "Just visiting."

"Sir," he said.

"You didn't say 'lieutenant' to me."

Sergeant Benet leaned over and looked at his name tag. "Afternoon, Captain Cox. Happy Thanksgiving, sir."

The captain didn't answer him. "Get out," he said.

"Get out, *Lieutenant*," I said. "Get out, *Sergeant*." But I got out, and so did Sergeant Benet, who came around the front of the truck and walked over to the captain. "Is there a problem, sir?"

The captain looked him up and down and said, "What've you got in there, Bennet?"

"Benet," Sergeant Benet said. "Like the writer, sir."

"What writer? What are you talking about?"

"Stephen Vincent Benét, sir."

"What did he write? Spirituals?"

The other MP, a private, shook his head: *Don't blame me.* The captain went to the back of the truck and lifted the canvas flap. Then he dropped it and walked up to the cab, where we had the Chicom jammed behind the seat. He found it right away. "Well, well, well," he said, "what have we here?" He turned the rifle over in his hands. "Very nice. Very nice indeed. Where'd you get it?"

"It's mine," I said, and reached out for it.

He pulled it back and showed me his teeth.

"Come on," I said. "Give it here."

"You're not allowed to bring enemy weapons onto this base. I'm taking this into custody pending a full investigation."

"In answer to your question, sir," Sergeant Benet said, "that rifle is a gift from our division commander, General Ngoc, to General Avery on the occasion of the American national holiday. General Avery is expecting it at this very moment. If you like, sir, I'll be more than happy to give him a call from the guard shack and let him explain the situation to you."

The captain looked at Sergeant Benet. I could see him trying to figure all this out, and I could see him give up. "Take the goddamn thing," he said, and pushed the rifle toward me. "Let this be a warning," he said.

"Sir, I apologize for the confusion," Sergeant Benet said.

After we drove away I asked Sergeant Benet just what he thought he was doing, taking a chance like that. Say the captain had actually gotten General Avery on the phone. Then what?

"That outstanding officer isn't going to bother a busy man like General Avery. Not on Thanksgiving, no sir. Never happen."

"But what if he did?"

"Well, sir, what do you think? You think the general's going to insult our Vietnamese hosts by turning down the offer of a number one gift like this?"

"As simple as that."

"Yes sir. I believe so, sir."

I followed the muddy track through the base. The base was nothing but mud and muddy tents and muddy men looking totally pissed off and brutal and demoralized. In their anger at being in this place and their refusal to come to terms with it they had created a profound, intractable bog. Something was wrong with the latrine system; the place always stank. They hadn't even bothered to plant any grass. At Dong Tam I saw something that wasn't allowed for in the national myth – our capacity for collective despair. People here seemed in the grip of unshakable petulance. It was in the slump of their shoulders and the plodding way they moved. A sourness had settled over the base, spoiling and coarsening the men. The resolute imperial will was all played out here at empire's fringe, lost in rancor and mud. Here were pharaoh's chariots engulfed; his horsemen confused; and all his magnificence dismayed.

A shithole.

Sergeant Benet and I stopped at the PX to buy a few things for Major Chau before going on to pick up the television. We sat down for some burgers and fries, then had seconds, then got lost in the merchandise, acres of stuff: cameras and watches and clothes, sound systems and perfume, liquor, jewelry, food, sporting equipment, bras, negligees. You could buy books. You could buy a trombone. You could buy insurance. You could buy a Hula-Hoop. They had a new car on display in the back of the store, a maroon GTO, with a salesman standing by to stroke the leather seats and explain its groundbreaking features, and to accept cut-rate, tax-free orders for this car or any other you might want – ready at your local dealer's on the scheduled date of your return home, with no obligation to anyone if, heaven forbid, some misfortune should prevent your return home.

We must have spent over an hour in there. We had the place almost to ourselves, and later, as we drove to the signal company where our TV was waiting, I noticed that the base itself seemed strangely empty, almost as if it had been abandoned. I smelled turkey baking. There must have been a bird in every oven in Dong Tam. The aroma contended with the stench of the latrines, and made me feel very far from home. That was always the effect of official attempts to make home seem closer.

We found Specialist Fourth Class Lyons playing chess

with another man in the company mess hall. They were both unshaven and wrecked-looking. Lyons took a pint bottle of Cutty Sark from under the table and offered it to us. Sergeant Benet waved it off and so did I. The argument against drinking and driving carried, on these roads, a persuasive new force.

"Where is everybody?" Sergeant Benet asked.

"Big show. Raquel Welch."

"Raquel Welch is here?"

"I think it's Raquel Welch." Lyons took a drink and gave the bottle to the other man. "Raquel Welch, right?"

"I thought it was Jill St John."

"Hey, maybe it's both of them, I don't know. Big difference. What with all the officers sitting up front you're lucky if you can even see the fucking stage. Seriously, man. They could have Liberace up there and you wouldn't know the difference, plus all the yahoos screaming their heads off."

"So," I said. "We've got the Chicom."

"Yeah, right. Oh boy. Problem time."

"Don't tell me about problems," Sergeant Benet said. "I didn't drive down here for any problems."

"I hear you, man. Really. The thing is, I couldn't swing it. Not for one Chicom."

"We agreed on one," I said. "That was the understanding."

"I know, I know. I'm with you, totally. It's just this guy, you know, my guy over there, he suddenly decides he wants two."

"He must be a crazy person," Sergeant Benet said. "Two Chicoms for a TV? He's crazy."

"I can get you some steaks. Fifty pounds."

"I don't believe this," I said. "We could've gotten killed coming down here."

"T-bone. Aged. This is not your average slice of meat," Lyons said.

The other man looked up from the chessboard. "I can vouch for that," he said. He kissed his fingertips.

"Or two Chicoms and I can get the TV," Lyons said. "I can have it for you in, like, an hour?"

"Who is this asshole?" I said. "Get him over here. We'll settle this right now."

"No can do. Sorry."

"We shook hands on this," Sergeant Benet said. "Don't you be jacking us around with this we-got-problems bullshit. Where's the TV?"

"I don't have it."

"Get it."

"Hey man, lighten up. It's not my fault, okay?"

Sergeant Benet turned and left the tent. I followed him.

"This is fucked," I said.

"We had a deal," Sergeant Benet said. "We shook hands."

We got in the truck and just sat there. "I can't accept this," I said.

"What I don't understand, that sorry-ass pecker-wood wanted two Chicoms, why didn't he *say* he wanted two Chicoms?"

"I refuse to accept this."

"Jack us around like that. *Shoot.*"

I told Sergeant Benet to drive up the road to an officers' lounge where I sometimes stopped for a drink. It was empty except for a Vietnamese woman washing glasses behind the bar. The TV was even bigger than I remembered, 25 inches, one of the custom Zeniths the army special-ordered for clubs and rec rooms. I motioned Sergeant Benet inside. The cleaning woman looked up as Sergeant Benet unplugged the TV and began disconnecting the aerial wire. "The picture is bad," I told her in Vietnamese. "We have to get it fixed."

She held the door open for us as we wrestled the TV outside.

On the way to the gate Sergeant Benet said, "What if Captain Cox is still moping around? What you going to do then?"

"He won't be."

"You better hope not, sir."

"Come on. You think he'd miss out on Raquel Welch?"

Captain Cox stepped outside the guard shack and waved us down.

"My God," I said.

"What you going to tell him?"

"I don't know."

"Then you best let me do the talking."

I didn't argue.

Captain Cox came up to the window and asked where we were headed now.

"Home, sir," Sergeant Benet said.

"Where's that?"

"Outside My Tho."

"Ah yes, you're with our noble allies."

"Yes sir."

"So what've you got in here?"

"Begging your pardon, sir, you already looked."

"Well, why don't I just take another look. Just for the heck of it."

"It's getting pretty late, sir. We don't want to be on the road come dark." Sergeant Benet nudged the accelerator.

"Turn off that engine," Captain Cox said. "Now you just damn well sit there until I say otherwise." He went around to the back of the truck, then came up to Sergeant Benet's window. "My," he said. "My, my, my, my, my."

"Listen," I said. But I couldn't think of anything else to say.

Sergeant Benet opened the door and got down from the cab. "If I could have a word with you, sir."

They walked off somewhere behind the truck. I heard Sergeant Benet talking but couldn't make out his words. Before long he came back and opened the door and pulled the Chicom from behind the seat. When he returned Captain Cox was with him. Captain Cox held the door as Sergeant Benet climbed inside, then closed it. "You boys have yourselves a good Thanksgiving now, hear?"

"Yes sir," Sergeant Benet said. "We'll do just that." And he drove out the gate.

"What a prick," I said.

"The captain? He's not so bad. He's a reasonable man. There's plenty that aren't."

Sergeant Benet pushed the truck hard, but he didn't look worried. He leaned into the corner and drove with one hand, his eyes hooded and vaguely yellow in the weak light slanting across the paddies. He smoked a Pall Mall without taking it from his lips, just letting it smolder and hang. He looked like a jazz pianist.

He was a hard one to figure out, Sergeant Benet. He thought it was amazing that I could get along in Vietnamese, but he spoke about ten different kinds of English, as occasion demanded – Cornerboy, Step'n'fetchit, Hallelujah Baptist, Professor of Cool, Swamp Runner, Earnest Oreo Professional; Badass Sergeant. The trouble I had understanding him arose from my assumption that his ability to run different numbers on other people meant that he would run numbers on me, but this hadn't proved out. With me he was always the same, a kind, dignified, forbearing man. He read the Bible every night before he went to bed. For wisdom he quoted his grandmother. Unlike me, he suffered no sense of corruption from his role as scrounge or from the extreme caution he normally practiced. He had survived Korea and a previous tour in Vietnam and he intended to survive this tour as well, without any romantic flourishes. He avoided personal talk, but I knew he was married and had several children, one of them a little girl with cerebral palsy. His wife was a cook in New Orleans.

He was solitary. His solitude was mostly of his own choosing, but not entirely. The Vietnamese had added our bigotries to their own, and now looked down on blacks along with Chinese, Montagnards, Lao, Cambodians, and other Vietnamese. If they had to have advisers they wanted white advisers, and they generally got what they wanted. Sergeant Benet was the only black adviser in the division. The Vietnamese didn't know what to make of him, because he gave no sign at all of being anybody's inferior. Even Major Chau deferred to him. Sergeant Benet sometimes got together in My Tho with a couple of sergeants from one of the other battalions. I had the idea they were out raising hell, until I saw them once in a bar downtown. Sergeant Benet was just sitting there, smoking, sipping his beer, looking into the distance while the other two talked and laughed.

The ferry had been almost empty on the way over, but when we got to the landing there was a long line for the crossing back. Two buses, two trucks full of vegetables, some scooters and mopeds, a whole bunch of people with bicycles. We were looking at three trips' worth, maybe more. Sergeant Benet went around the line and angled the truck in front of a bus. The driver didn't say anything. He was used to it. They were all used to it.

After we boarded the ferry Sergeant Benet settled back for a quick nap. He could do that, fall asleep at will. I got out and leaned against the rail and watched the ferryman wave the two buses into position, shouting, carving the air with his long, bony hands. The deck was packed with people. Old women with red teeth worked the crowd, selling rice balls, bread, fruit wrapped in wet leaves. Ducks paddled along the length of the hull, begging for crumbs. I could see their bills open and close but their calls were lost in the voices around me, the bark of the ferryman, the cries of the vendors, the blare of a tinny radio. The engine throbbed under the weathered planking.

A woman just down the rail was staring across the river, lost in thought. I recognized her immediately. A little boy, maybe five or six, stood between us, watching the ducks. I said hello to him in Vietnamese. He drew back against her, gave me a sober look, and did not answer. But I got what I wanted; she turned and saw me there. I greeted her in formal terms, and she had no choice but to return my greeting.

Her name was Anh. When I first got to My Tho she'd been working at division headquarters as a secretary and interpreter. One afternoon I stopped by her desk and tried to spark a conversation with her, but she had hardly lifted her eyes from the papers she was working on. She made me feel like a fool. Finally I gave up and went away without a word, knowing she wouldn't answer or even look up except to confirm that I really was leaving.

Then she lost her job, or quit. I hadn't seen her since, but sometimes her face came to mind – not very accurately, as it turned out.

Her face was covered with faint pale scars, subtle as the hairline veins under the glaze of old porcelain. They didn't spoil her looks, not as I saw her, and perhaps this is why I'd forgotten them. Their effect on me was to make me feel, in spite of the deliberate coldness of her gaze, that she was exposed and reachable. She had one small livid scar at the corner of her mouth. It curved slightly upward, giving her a lopsided, disbelieving smile. Her lips were full and vividly painted. I thought she might be Chinese; there were a lot of them in My Tho, traders and restaurateurs. She was paler and taller and heavier than most Vietnamese women, who in their floating ao dais seemed more spirit than flesh. Anh's neck swelled slightly above the high collar of her tunic. Her hands were white and plump. You could see the roundness of her arms under her taut sleeves.

Again in Vietnamese I asked the boy if he had been on

the bus. He looked at Anh. She told him to answer me. "Yes," he said, and looked back down at the ducks.

"Do you like riding the bus?"

"Answer him," Anh said.

He shook his head.

"You don't like the bus? Why not?"

He said something I didn't understand.

"He gets carsick," Anh said in English. "The roads are so bad now."

I wanted to keep the conversation in Vietnamese. In English I was accountable for what I said, but in Vietnamese I could be goofy or banal without having it held against me. In fact I had the idea that I was charming in Vietnamese.

To the boy I said, "Listen – this is true. Four times I took the bus across my own country. That's five thousand kilometers each way. Twenty thousand kilometers."

"Look," he said to Anh. "We're going."

So we were, slowly. The ducks didn't have any trouble keeping up.

"He's shy," Anh said in English.

Speaking English myself now, I said, "Is he shy with everyone? Or just me?"

"Just Americans."

"How come?"

She pushed out her lips and shrugged. It was something an actress would do in a French movie. She said, "He doesn't trust them."

"Why not?"

She shrugged again. "You're an American. Can he trust you?"

"Absolutely," I said.

She didn't say anything, but the other side of her mouth, the one without the scar, lifted slightly.

"What's his name?"

"Van."

"Your son?"

There was a change in her, and then she was looking at me without any friendliness at all. "My sister's," she said. "I take care of him. Sometimes." She turned away and leaned forward, elbows on the rail. She cocked one knee, then lifted the other foot and rubbed it up and down the back of her leg. I was supposed to think that I was no longer any part of her thoughts, but her movements were so calculated, so falsely spontaneous, that instead of discouraging me they gave me hope.

A wooden crate floated past with a bird perched on top. From out here on the river I could see how thick the trees grew on the banks, bristling right up to the edge and reaching out, trailing their branches in the water. Far above us a pair of jets flew silently. They were shining bright, brighter than anything down here, where the light was going out of the day.

"Hey, Van," I said.

He looked at me.

"Do you like TV?"

"Yes."

"What do you like to watch?"

He said something I didn't understand. I asked Anh for a translation. She took her time. Finally she turned and said, "It's a puppet show."

"How about *Bonanza*? You like *Bonanza*?"

"Little Joe," he said in English.

But he was already looking away.

"He doesn't see those shows," Anh said. "He hears about them from the other kids."

"Doesn't your sister let him?"

"No television," she said, and picked up the wicker bag at her feet. The drivers cranked their engines; people began to board the buses as we approached the landing. The trees cast long shadows out over the water, and when they fell over us the air turned cool, and Anh's face and hands took on the luminous quality of white things at dusk. I knew I had somehow made a fool of myself again. It vexed me, that and the way she'd smiled when I said I could be trusted. I made up my mind to show her I was a really good guy, not just another American blowhard.

"We have an extra TV," I said. "It's in the truck."

"We don't need television."

In Vietnamese, I said, "Van, do you want a television?"

"Yes," he said.

She hefted her bag. "What kind?"

"Zenith."

"Color?"

I nodded.

"How big?"

"Big enough."

"Nineteen inches?"

"Twenty-five."

"Twenty-five inches? How much?"

"It's not for sale."

"What for, then – Chicom?"

I couldn't help laughing.

"What for, then?"

33

"Nothing."

She watched me.

"It's a gift."

"A gift," she said. She went on watching me. She looked away and then looked at me again. "Okay," she said unhappily, as if agreeing to some exorbitant price.

I was going to tell her to forget about it if that was how she felt, but I said, "I can drop it off tonight."

She considered this. In a tone of surrender, she said, "Okay. Tonight." She told me where she lived. I knew the street – a line of cement-block bungalows along the reservoir, just inside town.

We let the buses go well ahead of us, figuring they'd pick up any mines that might have found their way into the road since we drove out. I didn't say anything to Sergeant Benet about my plans for the television until we approached the crossroads. A short distance to the west lay our battalion; a bit farther and to the east, My Tho. I asked him to make the turn east. "Let's get a drink," I said.

He wasn't interested. The drive back had done him in, and I knew how he felt because I wasn't exactly in the pink myself. We'd lost radio contact again after we left the landing. All we could get was static broken occasionally by urgent, indistinct voices that vanished when I tried to tune them in. The road was empty and getting dark. Stretches of it were already dark where trees overhung the road, scratching the top of the truck as we went by. Sergeant Benet had continued in his solitude, mute, pensive, not even smoking anymore. I'd been left with nothing for company but the consciousness of my own stupidity in making this trip, which I was now trying to talk Sergeant Benet into prolonging. Finally I had no choice but to tell him the truth, or a version of the truth in which I appeared as benefactor to a deprived child.

"What's his mother look like?"

"I don't know. I talked to his aunt."

"This aunt, she pretty?"

"I suppose you could say so."

"Well, sir, you didn't give away any TV."

"I'm afraid I did."

"No sir. It's still in the back there."

"But I promised." When he didn't say anything, I added, "I gave my word."

He turned west toward the battalion.

I could have made him drive the other direction, but I didn't. In this moment on the darkening road, Anh seemed a lot farther away than My Tho – an impossible distance. I was glad to be off the hook, and heading home to a good show.

We made it with time to spare. Sergeant Benet set up the television while I fried a couple of pork chops. He had trouble getting the color right; all the faces were yellow. I had a try at it and lost the picture completely, then gave him advice while he labored to get the picture back.

By the time *Bonanza* came on we were ready. We turned off the lights and settled in front of the screen, which looked like Cinerama after the dinky Magnavox we'd been watching. It was, as always, a story of redemption – man's innate goodness brought to flower by a strong dose of opportunity, hard work, and majestic landscape. During the scene when the wounded drifter whom Hoss has taken in (over Little Joe's objections) and nursed back to health nobly refuses, even under threat of death, to help his sociopath brother ambush the good brothers, the Cartwrights, and run off with their cattle, Sergeant Benet rocked in his seat and said, "Amen. Amen." He said it again during the big turkey-carving scene at the end, when the camera panned the happy faces at the Ponderosa feast table. And I was moved myself, as in some way I had planned to be. Why else would I have put myself on the road that afternoon except for the certain reward of this emotion, unattainable from a 12-inch black-and-white? — this swelling of pride in the beauty of my own land, and the good hearts and high purposes of her people, of whom, after all, I was one.

Command Presence

When I was eighteen I worked on a ship, a Coast and Geodetic Survey ship out of Norfolk. As I sat on my bunk one night, reading a book, I became aware that one of my shipmates was staring at me. My face burned, the words started swimming on the page, the tranquillity in which I had been imagining the scenes of the novel was broken. For a time I blindly regarded the book and listened to the voices of the other men, the long shuddering surge of the engine. Finally I had no choice but to look back at him.

He was one of the ship's mechanics. He had rabbity eyes and red hair cropped so close his scalp showed through. His skin was white. Not fair. White, the pallor of a life spent belowdecks. He hardly ever spoke. I had felt the weight of his scrutiny before, but never like this. I saw that he hated me.

Why did he hate me? He may have felt – I might have made him feel – that I was a tourist here, that my life would not be defined, as his had been, by years of hard labor at sea relieved now and then by a few days of stone drunkenness in the bars of Norfolk and Newport News. I'd been down to the engine room on errands and maybe he'd seen me there and seen the fastidiousness that overcame me in this dim, clanking, fetid basement where half-naked men with greasy faces loomed from the shadows, shouting and brandishing wrenches. He might have noted my distaste and taken it as an affront. Maybe my looks rubbed him wrong, or my manner of speech, or my habitual clowning and wising off, as if we were all out here on a lark. I was cheerful to a fault, no denying that; glib, breezy, heedless of the fact that for most of the men this cramped inglorious raft was the end of the line. It could have been that. Or it could have been the book I was reading, the escape the book represented at that moment and in time to come. Then again there might have been no particular reason for what he felt about me. Hatred sustains itself very well without benefit of cause.

Not knowing what to think of him, I thought nothing at all. I lived in a dream anyway, in which I featured then as a young Melville, my bleary alcoholic shipmates as bold, vivid characters with interesting histories they would one day lay bare to me. Most of what I looked at I didn't really see, and this mechanic was part of what I didn't see.

I worked on cleanup details in the morning, scraped and painted in the afternoon. One day I was scraping down the hull of a white runabout that was kept on davits for the captain's pleasure and as a partial, insincere fulfillment of our lifeboat requirement. It was sultry. The sun beat down through a white haze that dazzled the eyes. I ducked under the boat and pretended to take an interest in the condition of the keel. It was cool there in the shadows. I leaned back, my head resting against one of the propeller blades, and closed my eyes.

I slept for a while. When I woke I felt heavy and dull, but I couldn't go back to sleep. In this muzzy state I heard someone stop beside me, then walk to the stern. I opened my eyes and saw a pair of bell-bottom pant legs ascending the ladder. Boards creaked overhead. My nap was done.

I sat up and shook my head, waited for clarity, was still sitting there when a great roar went up behind me. I looked back and saw the propeller I'd just had my head on spinning in a silver blur. I scuttled out from under the boat, got to my feet, and looked up at the mechanic, who was watching me from the gunwale of the runabout. Neither of us said a word. I knew I should go after him, even if it meant taking a beating. But he was ready to kill me. This was a new consideration, and one that gave me pause, excessive pause. I stood there and let him face me down until he decided to turn away.

I didn't know what to do. He'd given me no evidence for a complaint to the captain. If I accused him, the mechanic would say it was an accident, and then the captain would ask me what the hell I was doing down there anyway, lying against a propeller. It *was* pretty stupid. That's what my shipmates told me, the two of them I trusted enough to talk things over with. But they believed me, they said, and promised to keep an eye on him. This sounded good, at first. Then I understood that it meant nothing. He would choose the time and place, not them. I was on my own.

The ship put in a few days later to take on supplies for a trip to the Azores. The weekend before our departure, I went to Virginia Beach with another man and ended up on the first dark hours of Monday morning propped against the seawall, trying to make myself get up and walk the half mile to the motel where my shipmate was waiting for me. In an hour or so he'd have to begin the drive back to Norfolk or risk having the ship weigh anchor without him. I sat there in the chilly blow, trembling with cold and sunburn, and hugged my knees and waited for the sun to rise. Everything was cloaked in uncongenial grayness, not only the sky but also the water and the beach, where gulls walked to and fro with their heads pulled down between their wings. A band of red light appeared on the horizon.

This was not the unfolding of any plan. I'd never intended to miss my ship, not once, not for a moment. It was the first cruise to foreign waters since I'd been on board, and I wanted to go. In the Azores, according to a book I'd read, they still harpooned whales from open boats. I had already made up my mind to get in on one of these hunts, no matter what. All my shipmates had the bug, even the old tars who should've known better. When they said "Azores" their voices cradled the word. They were still subject to magic, still able at the sound of a name – *Recife, Dakar, Marseilles* – to see themselves not as galley slaves but as adventurers to whom the world was longing to offer itself up.

I didn't want to miss my ship. Forget about far-off places, the open sea; the ship was my job, and I had no prospects for another. I didn't even have a high school diploma. The prep school I'd finagled my way into had tolerated my lousy grades and fatuous contempt for its rules until, in my senior year, having pissed away my second and third and fourth chances, I was stripped of my scholarship and launched upon the tide of affairs, to sink or swim. I appeared to be sinking.

Where to turn? My mother lived in one small room in Washington, D.C., where she worked as a secretary by day, by night as a restaurant hostess. She had just begun to accord me, with touching eagerness, the signs of respect due a man who pulled his own weight in the world. Unteachable optimist that she was, she drew hope from every glint of gravity in my nature, every possibility of dealing with me as an equal. I didn't want to think about the look on her face when I turned up at her door with some tomfool story about the ship sailing without me. Where else, then? My brother Geoffrey and I were good friends. He might have been open to a visit except that he was in England, doing graduate work at Cambridge on a Fulbright fellowship. His good luck; my bad luck. My father was also unable to play host at just this moment, being in jail in California, this time for passing bad checks under the name Sam Colt.

I had to join my ship. But I stayed where I was. People with dogs began to appear on the beach. Old folks collecting driftwood. When there was no longer any chance of meeting my shipmate I got up stiffly and walked into town, where I ate a jumbo breakfast and pondered the army recruiting office across the street.

This wasn't a new idea, the army. I'd always known I would wear the uniform. It was essential to my idea of legitimacy. The men I'd respected when I was growing up had all served, and most of the writers I looked up to – Norman Mailer, Irwin Shaw, James Jones, Erich Maria Remarque, and of course Hemingway, to whom I turned for guidance in all things. Military service was not an incidental part of their histories; they were unimaginable apart from it. I wanted to be a writer myself, had described myself as one to anybody who would listen since I was sixteen. It was laughable for a boy my age to call himself a writer on the evidence of two stories in a school lit mag, but improbable as this self-conception was, it nevertheless changed my way of looking at the world. The life around me began at last to take on form, to signify. No longer a powerless confusion of desires, I was now a protagonist, the hero of a novel to which I endlessly added from the stories I dreamed and saw everywhere. The problem was, I began to see stories even where I shouldn't, where what was required of me was simple fellow feeling. I turned into a predator, and one of the things I became predatory about was experience. I fetishized it, collected it, kept strict inventory. It seemed to me the radical source of authority in the writers whose company I wanted to join, in spite of their own coy deference to the ugly stepsisters honesty, knowledge, human sympathy, historical consciousness, and, ugliest of all, hard work. They were just being polite. Experience was the clapper in the bell, the money in the bank, and of all experiences the most bankable was military service.

I had another reason for considering this move. I wanted to be respectable, to take my place one day among respectable men. Partly this was out of appetite for the things respectable men enjoyed, things even the dimmest of my prep school classmates could look forward to as a matter of course. But that wasn't all of it, or even most of it. My father's career, such as it was – his unflinching devolution from ace airplane designer to welsher, grifter, convict – appalled me. I had no sense of humor about it. Nor, for all my bohemian posturing, did it occur to me to see him as some kind of hero or saint of defiance against bourgeois proprieties. He had ruined his good name, which happened to be my name as well. When people asked me about my father I sometimes told them he was dead. In saying this I did not feel altogether a liar. To be dishonored and at the end of your possibilities – was that life? He appalled me and frightened me, because I saw in myself the same tendencies that had brought him to grief.

The last time I'd lived with my father was the summer of my fifteenth year, before I went back east to school. We were taking a walk one night and stopped to admire a sports car in a used car lot. As if it were his sovereign right, my father reached inside and popped the hood open and began to explain the workings of the engine, which was similar to that of the Abarth-Allemagne he was then driving (unpaid for, never to be paid for). As he spoke he took a knife from his pocket and cut the gas line on either side of the filter, which he shook out and wrapped in a handkerchief, talking all the while. It was exactly the kind of thing I would have done, but I hated seeing him do it, as I hated seeing him lie about his past and bilk storekeepers and take advantage of his friends. He had crooked ways, the same kind I had, but after that summer I tried to change. I didn't want to be like him. I wanted to be a man of honor.

Honor. The very word had a martial ring. My father had never served, though he sometimes claimed he had, and this incompleteness in his history somehow made his fate intelligible and offered a means to escape it myself. This was the way, the indisputable certificate of citizenship and probity.

But I didn't join up that morning. Instead I went to Washington to bid my mother farewell, and let her persuade me to have another try at school, with results so dismal that in the end she personally escorted me to the recruiter.

I never made it to the Azores, and even now the word raises a faint sensation of longing and regret. But I was right not to go back to my ship that morning. So many things can happen at sea. You can go overboard at night. Something heavy can fall on you, or something sharp. You can have your hat size reduced by a propeller. A ship is a dangerous place at any time; but when one of your shipmates wishes you harm, then harm is certain to befall you. In that way a ship is like a trapeze act, or a family, or a company of soldiers.

I went through basic training at Fort Jackson, South Carolina, during a heat wave, "the worst on record," we kept telling one another, on no authority but our opinion that it was pretty damned hot. And it was. The asphalt streets liquefied, sucking at our boots, burning our eyes and throats with acrid fumes. Sweat gleamed on every face. When they packed us into Quonset huts for lectures on "homoseshality" and "drug addition," the smell got serious enough to put a man down, and many went down. Passing out came to be so common among us that we awarded points for the drama of the fall. The big winner was a boy from Puerto Rico who keeled over while marching, in full field equipment, along a ledge on a steep hillside. We heard him clanking all the way down.

The drill sergeants affected not to be aware of the rate at which we dropped. They let us understand that taking notice of the temperature was unsoldierly. When a recruit in another company died of heatstroke, our company commander called a formation and told us to be sure and take our salt pills every day. After he'd given his speech and gone back to the orderly room, our drill sergeant said, "Shitbirds, why did that troop croak?"

We had the answer ready. "Because he was a pussy, Sergeant."

We were mostly volunteers. A lot of men regretted the impulse that had brought them to Fort Jackson, and all of us whined unceasingly, but I never heard of anyone writing to his congressman about the treatment we got, which was pretty much what a boy brought up on war movies would expect, and maybe a little better. The drill sergeants rode us hard, but they didn't show up drunk at midnight and lead us into swamps to drown. The training seemed more or less purposeful, most of the time. The food was decent. And there were pleasures to be had.

One of my pleasures was to learn that I was hardy and capable. I'd played team sports in school, and played them doggedly, but never very well. Military training agreed with me. My body was right for it – trim and stringy. Guys who would have pulverized me on the football field were still on their third push-up when I'd finished my tenth. The same bruisers had trouble on our runs and suffered operatically on the horizontal bar, where we had to do pull-ups before every meal. Their beefy bodies, all bulked up for bumping and bashing, swayed like carcasses under their white-knuckled hands. Their necks turned red, their arms quivered, they grunted piteously as they tried to raise their chins to the bar. They managed to pull themselves up once or twice and then just hung there, sweating and swearing. Now and then they kicked feebly. Their pants slipped down, exposing pimply white butts. Those of us who'd already done our pull-ups gathered around to watch them, under the pretense of boosting their morale ("Come on, Moose!'You can do it! One more, Moose! One more for the platoon!") but really to enjoy their misery, and perhaps to reflect, as I did, on the sometimes perfect justice turned out by fortune's wheel.

Instead of growing weaker through the long days I felt myself taking on strength. Part of this strength came from contempt for weakness. Before now I'd always felt sorry for people who had trouble making the grade. But here a soft heart was an insupportable luxury, and I learned that lesson in smart time.

We had a boy named Sands in our squad, one of several recruits from rural Georgia. He had a keen, determined look about him that he used to good advantage for a couple of weeks, but it wasn't enough to get him by. He was always lagging behind somewhere. Last to get up. Last to formation. Last to finish eating. Our drill sergeant was from Brooklyn, and he came down hard on this cracker who didn't take his army seriously.

Sands seemed not to care. He was genial and sunny even in the face of hostility, which I took to be a sign of grit. I liked him and tried to help. When he fell out on runs I hung back with him a few times to carry his rifle and urge him on. But I began to realize that he wasn't really trying to keep up. When a man is on his last legs you can hear it in the tearing hoarseness of every breath. It's there in his rolling eyes, in his spastically jerking hands, in the way he keeps himself going by falling forward and making his feet hurry to stay under him. But Sands grinned at me and wagged his head comically: *Jeez Louise, where's the fire?* He wasn't in pain. He was coasting. It came as a surprise to me that Sands would let someone else pull his weight before he was all used up.

There were others like him. I learned to spot them, and to stay clear of them, and finally to mark my progress by their humiliations. It was a satisfaction that took some getting used to, because I was soft and because it contradicted my values, or what I'd thought my values to be. Every man my brother: that was the idea, if you could call it an idea. It was more a kind of attitude that I'd picked up, without struggle or decision, from the movies I saw, the books I read. I'd paid nothing for it and didn't know what it cost.

It cost too much. If every man was my brother we'd have to hold our lovefest some other time. I let go of that notion, and the harshness that took its place gave me a certain power. I was recognized as having "command presence" – arrogance, an erect posture, a loud, barky voice. They gave me an armband with sergeant's stripes and put me in charge of the other recruits in my platoon. It was like being a trusty.

I began to think I could do anything. At the end of boot camp I volunteered for the airborne. They trained me as a radio operator, then sent me on to jump school at Fort Benning, Georgia. When I arrived, my company was marched onto the parade ground in a cold rain and drilled and dropped for push-ups over the course of the evening until we were covered with mud and hardly able to stand, at which time they sent us back inside and ordered us to be ready for inspection in thirty minutes. We thought we were, but they didn't agree. They dumped our footlockers onto the floor, knocked our wall lockers down, tore up our bunks, and ordered us outside again for another motivational seminar. This went on all night. Toward morning, wet, filthy, weaving on my feet as two drill sergeants took turns yelling in my face, I looked across the platoon bay at the morose rank of men waiting their ration of abuse, and saw in one mud-caked face a sudden lunatic flash of teeth. The guy was *grinning*. At *me*. In complicity, as if he knew me, had always known me, and knew exactly how to throw the switch that turned the most miserable luck, the worst degradations and prospects, into my choicest amusements. Like this endless night, this insane, ghastly scene. Wonderful! A scream! I grinned back at him. We were friends before we ever knew each other's names.

His name was Hugh Pierce. He was from Philadelphia. It turned out that we'd gone to rival prep schools. To come across anyone from that life here was strange enough, but I didn't give the coincidence much thought. We hardly ever talked about our histories. What had happened to us up to then seemed beside the point. Histories were what we'd joined the army to have.

For three weeks the drill sergeants harried us like wolves, alert to any sign of weakness. Men started dropping out. Hugh loved it. The more fantastic the oppressions, the greater his delight. He couldn't stop himself from grinning his wiggy grin, bouncing on the balls of his feet as he waited for the next absurdity. Whenever the drill sergeants caught him smiling they swarmed all over him, shouted dire threats directly into his ears, made him do push-ups while they sat on his back. Nothing got to him. His pleasure in the ridiculous amounted almost to a pathology. And they couldn't wear him down, he was too strong for that

— immensely strong, and restless in his strength. Unlike me, Hugh made a habit of helping men who dropped back on our runs, mostly out of generosity, but also because to him exertion was joy. He liked making it harder for himself, pushing the limits however he could. At night, when the last drill instructor had exacted the last push-up and pronounced the last insult, we fell into our bunks and made wisecracks until sleep got us. But for me the joke was wearing a little thin. By now I was mainly trying to keep up.

In the last week we jumped. We jumped every day. For hours each morning we waited on the tarmac, running in place, doing push-ups and equipment checks while the drill sergeants went through all the possibilities of getting lunched. They dwelt in loving detail on the consequence to our tender persons of even the slightest accident or mistake. Did anyone want to reconsider? Just step to the side. Always, some did. Then we boarded the planes, facing one another across the aisle until the green light came on and the jumpmaster gave the order to stand and hook up our static lines. To psych ourselves for the plunge we sang "My Girl" in falsetto and danced the Stroll, swinging our shoulders and hips, flapping our wrists feyly as we made our way down the cargo bay to the open door of the plane. The planes were C-130 turboprops. The prop blast was tremendous, and you jumped right into it. It caught you and shot you back feetfirst spinning like a bullet. You could see the earth and sky whirling around your boots like painted sections on a top. Then the chute snapped open and stopped you cold, driving your nuts into your belly if you didn't have the harness set right, snatching you hard even if you did. The pain was welcome, considering the alternative. It was life itself grabbing hold of you. You couldn't help but laugh – some of us howled. The harness creaked as you swung back and forth under the luminous white dome of the silk. Other chutes bloomed in the distance. The air was full of men, most quiet, some yelling and working their risers to keep from banging into each other. The world was laid out at your feet: checkered fields, shining streams and ponds, cute little houses. For a time you belonged to the air, weightless and free; then the earth took you back. You could feel it happen. One moment you were floating, the next you were falling – not a pleasant change. The ground, abstractly picturesque from on high, got hard-looking and particular. There were trees, boulders, power lines. It seemed personal, even vengeful, the way these things rushed up at you. If you were lucky you landed in the drop zone and made a good rolling fall, then quick-released your parachute before it could drag you and break your neck. As you gathered in the silk you looked up and watched the next stick of troopers make the leap, and the sight was so mysterious and beautiful it was impossible not to feel love for this life. It seemed, at such a moment, the only possible life, and these men the only possible friends.

In our last week of jump school Hugh and I signed up for the Special Forces and were sent on to Fort Bragg.

The Special Forces came out of the OSS teams of World War II. They'd worked in German-occupied territory, leading partisan brigades, blowing bridges and roads, killing enemy officers. The membership was international. When I came to Fort Bragg some of the old hands were still around:

Czechs, Poles, Ukrainians, Brits, Hungarians. We also had a number of Germans who had signed on after the war, more attached to the uniformed life than to any homeland.

This accented remnant gave a legionary feeling to the unit, but most of the troops were young and American. They were also tough and smart, and savvy in a way that I began to understand I was not. I could keep up with them physically, but I didn't get the hang of things as easily as they did – as if they'd been born knowing how to lay a mortar, blow a bridge, bushwhack through blind undergrowth without ever losing their sense of where they were. Though I could do a fair impersonation of a man who knew his stuff, the act wouldn't hold up forever. One problem was that I didn't quite believe in it myself.

There was no single thing I had trouble with, no skill I couldn't eventually learn. I simply ceased to inhabit my pose. I was at a distance, watching this outrageous fraud play the invisible bushman, the adept with knives, the black-faced assassin willing at the drop of a hat to squeeze the life out of some total stranger with piano wire. And in that widening distance between the performance and the observation of the performance, there grew, subtly at first, then intrusively, disbelief and corrosive irony. It was a crisis, but I hardly recognized its seriousness until one achingly pure spring day at the sawdust pit where we practiced hand-to-hand combat.

We were on a smoke break. I lay on my back, staring up at the sky. Our two instructors were sitting behind me on the wall of sandbags that surrounded the pit. One of them had just received orders for Vietnam and was saying he wouldn't go back, not this time. He'd already done two six-month tours, and that, he said, was enough. The other sergeant murmured commiseration and said he could protest the orders but it probably wouldn't do any good. He didn't seem at all surprised by this show of reluctance, or even falsely sympathetic. He sounded troubled. I'm not going, the sergeant with the orders kept saying. I'm not going.

Both of them were dull the rest of the session. They just went through the motions.

This set me thinking. Here you had a man who knew all the tricks and knew them well enough to teach them to others. He'd been there twice and been competent enough to get home. Yet he was afraid. He was afraid and didn't bother to hide it from another man who'd been there, certain it wouldn't be held against him. What sort of knowledge did they share, to have reached this understanding?

And if this sergeant, who was the real thing, had reason to be afraid, what about me? What would happen when my accounts came due and I had to be in truth the wily, nerveless killer I pretended to be? It was not my habit to meditate on this question. It came to me unbidden, breaking through the bluff imitation of adequacy I tried so hard to believe in.

I never unloaded my worries on Hugh. I didn't hide them, but when we were out on a tear they ceased to trouble me. We patrolled Fayetteville on our nights off and spent the weekends cruising farther afield in Hugh's Pontiac, to Myrtle Beach and Chapel Hill and down to Fort Gordon, Georgia, where his brother was stationed. Yak, yak, yak, all the way. Girls. The peculiarities of our brothers-in-arms. Books – at least I talked about books.

And of course the future. We had big plans. After we got out of the army we were going to get all our friends together and throw the party of the century. We were going to buy motorcycles and bazooka through Europe. We were going to *live*. It's been almost thirty years now and the words are mostly gone, but I remember the ecstatic rush of them, and the laughter. I could make Hugh laugh pretty much at will. It was a sight: crimson circles appeared on his high cheeks, his eyes brightened with tears, he wheezed for breath. He could do the same thing to me. We were agreed that the world was a comical place, and that we'd been put here for the sacred purpose of being entertained by it.

And we sang; how we sang. Hugh had uncanny rhythm. He could do scat. He could imitate a bass, a muted trumpet. He had a good voice but preferred to sing harmony and backup while I took the lead. We did old Mills Brothers songs, the Ink Spots, Sinatra. A couple of the girls we went out with were always after us for "The Best Is Yet to Come." That was our big gun. I laid down the melody while Hugh did crazy riffs around it, shoulders jumping, eyes agleam, head weaving like a cobra's. We might have been pretty good. Then again, maybe we weren't.

This was 1965. The air force had started bombing North Vietnam in February. The marines were in Danang, and the army had forty-four combat battalions on the way. Plenty of guys we knew were packing up for the trip. Hugh and I were going too, no question about that, but we never talked about the war. I can guess now that the reckless hilarity of our time together owed something to our forebodings, but I didn't suspect that at the time. Neither of us acknowledged being afraid, not to each other. What good would that do? We had chosen this life. My reasons were personal rather than patriotic, but I had consented to be made use of, and in spite of my fears it never occurred to me, nor I'm sure to Hugh, that we would be used stupidly or carelessly or for unworthy ends. Our trust was simple, immaculate, heartbreaking.

That fall Hugh got sent for medic's training to Fort Sam Houston in Texas. I was at loose ends and bored. My company commander had been working on me to apply for Officer Candidate School, and I finally agreed. I took some tests and went before a panel of generals and colonels who took note of my command presence and pronounced me officer material. They told me I'd be on my way in a month or so.

While I was awaiting my orders I got a letter from one of the girls Hugh had gone out with. Her name was Yancy. She said she was pregnant and that Hugh was the father. She knew he'd left Fort Bragg but didn't know where to find him, and asked me to send her his address and let him know the situation. I got this letter on a Saturday afternoon. The building was empty. I sat on my bunk and tried to think what to do. Yancy was the friend of a girl named Trace I'd gone out with. The two of them roomed together, tending bar and living it up on terms as hedonistic as ours, or so it seemed to me. I hadn't seen either of them since Hugh left, and I didn't know what to make of this. Was I honestly supposed to believe that Hugh was the only man Yancy had been close to during the time in question? I supposed it was just possible. But what would Hugh think if I gave her his address, or if I sent him the message she wanted me to send? Would he think I was meddling, taking her side?

Judging him? I understand that the strongest friendship can be spoiled by a word, a tone, even an imagined one.

Why had she written me, anyway? It didn't matter where he was, if she'd addressed the letter to Hugh it would have been forwarded. Maybe she didn't know his last name. Did he not want her to know?

I put the letter away. I would consider it, then come to a decision. But I never could decide. The standard by which Hugh and I tried to live was loyalty, and I'd always thought it was a good one. In the face of the Other we closed ranks. That worked fine when the Other was a bullying sergeant or a bunch of mouthy drunks, but it didn't shed much light here, where she was a girl in trouble. I could sense the insufficiency of the code but had no stomach for breaking it, at the risk of betraying Hugh. In the end I did nothing. I let other matters claim my attention.

My orders came. Instead of sending me to the infantry school at Fort Benning, they assigned me to artillery Officer Candidate School at Fort Sill, Oklahoma. I felt both guilty and relieved. Since the Special Forces had no howitzers they could not reasonably send me back there. My logic was impeccable, but six months later, with twenty years of life under my belt and new gold bars on my shoulders, I opened my orders and saw that I was going right back where I started, to Fort Bragg and the Special Forces.

My position was absurd. While laboring to become an artilleryman I had acquired a body of skills now utterly useless to me – trigonometry! calculus! – and lost or grown clumsy in those I needed. It was going to be hard for the troops at Fort Bragg to take me seriously as an officer when some of them had known me not long before as an enlisted man, and as something of a fuck-up. I couldn't even take myself seriously. In my OCS class I'd finished forty-ninth out of forty-nine, the class goat – like Custer, as no one lost a chance to tell me.

It wasn't as disgraceful as it looked. There'd been one hundred twenty of us to start with. But it was still pretty bad. I barely passed the gunnery course, and then only by pulling all-nighters in the latrine. I was chronically late and unkempt. My jocose manner amused only a few of my classmates and none of my training officers, who in their reports labeled me "extraneous" and "magic" – not a compliment in those circles – and never failed to include me in the weekly Jark, an hours-long punishment run in full field equipment, which was so effective in producing misery that people used to line the streets to watch us stumble past, as they would have gathered to watch a hanging. Some bystanders were actually moved to pity by the sight of us, and slipped us candy bars and words of encouragement. The true Christians among them threw water on our heads.

In the end I finished OCS only because, mainly to amuse myself, I had written a number of satirical songs and sketches for our battery to perform on graduation night. These revues, in the style of Hasty Pudding or the Princeton Triangle, were a tradition at Fort Sill and a big headache to our training officers, whose talents did not lie in this direction. Along with hundreds of other visitors, the post commandant and his staff would be in attendance. There'd be hell to pay if the show was a flop. When the time came for the final cuts to be made in our class it was discovered that I was the only one who could put the whole thing together.

They kept me on to produce a farce. That was how I became an officer in the United States Army.

One by one Hugh and my other buddies disappeared into the war. I kept waiting for my own orders. At last I did get orders, but instead of Vietnam they sent me to the Defense Language Institute in Washington, D.C., to study Vietnamese for a year. Most of the students were young Foreign Service officers. So I wouldn't stick out too much, I was detached from the army and put on civilian status. I could live where I wanted to live. I reported to no one, and no one checked up on me. My only duty was to learn Vietnamese. On top of my regular salary I got per diem for food, housing, and civilian clothes. Before leaving Fort Bragg I was issued a pamphlet showing in detail the kind of mufti an officer should wear on different occasions, from clambakes to weddings. Each "Correct" picture was paired with an "Incorrect" picture – goateed beatniks in shades and sandals, hipsters in zoot suits, doughy proles in bermudas and black socks. The correct guys always wore dark blue suits except when they were doing their morning run.

It wasn't a hardship post. My mother still lived in Washington and so did my brother, Geoffrey, and his wife, Priscilla. I had some good friends in town as well, guys I'd known from school days and kept in touch with during my leaves home. Laudie Greenway, in town for a last fling before joining the army himself. George Crile, studying at Georgetown and working as a stringer for Drew Pearson. Bill Treanor, about to open the first home in Washington for runaway kids. We threw in together and rented a house not far from Dupont Circle. Our landlady was Jeane Dixon, the newspaper sibyl who'd become famous by predicting the deaths of President Kennedy and Dag Hammarskjöld. She collected the rent in person, but not from me. As soon as her car pulled up I went running out the back door before she had a chance to see me and start prophesying. In all the time I lived there I never once let her lay eyes on me.

I bought a Volkswagen and took girls to Wolf Trap and the Cellar Door. I smoked dope. I began a novel, which, somewhat to my surprise, I managed to work on in a fairly disciplined way. I fell in love.

Her name was Vera. She was related by marriage to a Russian prince, and had grown up among expatriate Russians and come to think of herself as one of them. She had their wounded gaiety, their air of romantic, genteel displacement, their manners and terms of address. Her grandfather she called Opa; her brother Gregory, Grisha. She hated to cook, but when she had no choice she made great borscht. She favored high boots and bright skirts and scarves such as a Russian princess might wear while at leisure among her beloved serfs, picking mushrooms or hunting bears or dancing to the balalaika. She drank like a man and ate like a wolf. I fell in love with her the first night I saw her and pursued her for weeks afterward. I loved her name, her odd swinging stride, her dark wit and mad laugh, her clothes, her pale skin and antique, heart-shaped face. She had a steady boyfriend but I kept after her anyway until finally she surprised us both by falling in love with me. Her best friend, the girl who'd introduced us, took me aside and told me I was in way over my head. I didn't know what she was talking about, but I began to learn.

She could be very funny, my Vera, but her humor was desperate and biting. She was obsessed by a single terrible truth, that everything and everyone you love will someday be taken from you. For Vera all other truths were frivolous; this was the one that mattered. Her father had been her closest friend. He had told her his secrets. They had conducted ESP experiments together – successfully, according to Vera. She had lost him suddenly, without any warning, when she was in her first year of boarding school, and the pain that came upon her then had never left her. She saw everything through it.

And as if it weren't enough by itself, this unhealing wound was endlessly abraded by anger, anger at the world for being a place where such a thing could happen. She wouldn't have said so herself, but her father's death left her feeling deserted. And because she was convinced that everyone else would desert her in the end, she was always looking for the first signs. Just about everything was a sign. A quizzical look, failure to agree; reference to experience not shared with her, private sorrow, old loyalties. Anything could qualify. And her rage at such betrayals was uncontainable.

We were driving across the Chesapeake Bay Bridge late one night. It was hot in the car, and I asked Vera to crack the window. She looked at me curiously. I asked her again. *What?* she said. *Crack the window?* Please, I said. She screamed *Here!* and struck the windshield with the heel of her hand. She did it again, and again, as hard as she could. *Here! Here!* I grabbed her wrist so she wouldn't hurt herself and asked what I'd done wrong. *You know*, she said. She stared ahead, hugging herself. Finally she declared she'd never in her life heard the expression "crack the window," and said further that I *knew* she'd never heard it. Why, she asked, did I like to mock her? Exactly what pleasure did it give me?

I thought it best not to answer, but my silence goaded her to fury, and the injured sound of her own voice served as proof that I had wronged her, that I was vicious, disloyal, unworthy, hateful. Vera was still going strong when we got to my place. She hadn't moved in with me yet; that opera had yet to open. My friends and I lived in a black neighborhood where people didn't observe the white protocol of seeming not to hear what was going on around them. I tried to hush Vera but she was in full cry, and before long our neighbors joined in, yelling at us from up and down the street. They were inspirational to Vera but not to me. I told her she had to go home, and when she refused I simply got out of my car and went inside.

It was well after midnight. My friends were in their rooms, gallantly pretending to be asleep. I opened a beer and carried it to the living room.

The first crash wasn't that loud. It sounded like someone had kicked over a garbage can. The second was louder. I went to the window and parted the blinds. Vera was backing down the street in her mother's old Mercedes. This was a blocky gray diesel made, no doubt, from melted-down panzers. Vera went about fifty feet, stopped, ground the gears, started up the street again and rammed my car head-on, caving in the hood. Her undercarriage got caught on my bumper as she pulled away. She couldn't move but kept trying anyhow, racing the engine, rending metal. Then she popped the clutch and the engine died.

"I'm going to kill you," I told her when I reached the street.

I must have looked like I meant it, because she locked her door and sat there without saying a word. I walked back and forth around my car, a yellow Volkswagen bug, the first car I'd ever owned. It was cherry when I bought it. An unusual word to use about a VW, but that's what the ad said: "Cherry, needs tires, runs good." Gospel, every word. It was a good car but a soft car, no match for the armor-plated *Überauto* now parked on its hood. Before landing there Vera had nailed the bug twice on the driver's side, caving in the door and breaking the window.

I kept circling it. As I walked I began to tote up the damage, translating it into words that offered some hope of amendment. *Crumpled fender. Dents on door panel.* A phrase came to mind that I tried to dismiss and forget, because the instant I thought of it I knew it would undo me. *Cracked window.* I sat down on the curb. Vera got out of her car. She walked over, sat beside me, leaned against my shoulder.

"You cracked the window," I said. "I'll think twice before I ask you to do that again." And we sat there laughing at my ruined car.

This sort of thing became routine, all in a day's work. At first I was able to see Vera's fits as aristocratic peculiarity, and even managed to believe that I could somehow deliver her from them and help her become as squared away as I was. After all, she looked as solid as a rock compared to her brother Grisha.

I never actually met Grisha. Just before I started going out with Vera he had quarreled with their mother over something so trivial she couldn't remember it afterward, except that she had said something about not liking the look on his face, whereupon Grisha declared that he wouldn't inflict his face on her or anyone else ever again, and locked himself in his room upstairs. He refused to come out except when there was no one to see him. Vera's mother left Grisha's meals on a tray outside his door and carried the dirty dishes away when he was done. The same with his laundry. That was the situation when I first visited the house. Vera's mother was a fond and patient woman who had long ago surrendered her authority in the family. She accepted this business with Grisha as she accepted everything her children did. Anyway, it couldn't go on much longer. Summer was almost over. Grisha had another year of school left, and he would have to leave the room once classes began.

That's what she thought, but Grisha thought otherwise. Just before Labor Day he left a note with his dirty dishes announcing that he planned to stay right where he was and get his diploma by correspondence. He trusted his mother to arrange the details.

She called a family council to discuss the question, and asked me to sit in. I was glad to do it. It was a sign of favor and I did my best to be worthy of it. When she asked for my view I gave sound military advice, which was to lay siege to Grisha. Starve the brat out, I told her. She had to show him he wasn't the center of the universe.

When I finished I looked at Vera's mother and saw that I'd been wrong: Grisha *was* the center of the universe.

She seemed embarrassed and a little amazed that I didn't know this. She thanked me and turned to Vera, then the talk turned serious. They reasoned together and after sober consideration reached their decision. Grisha could do anything he wanted to do.

Vera's mother signed him up for correspondence school and continued to minister to him. But one night Grisha opened his door just as she was picking up his dinner tray. For a breathless moment they were face-to-face. Then Grisha slammed the door and immediately took measures to ensure that no such accident ever happened again. He wrapped his head completely in gauze, leaving little holes for his mouth, eyes, ears, and nostrils. Once he was all covered up he became less reclusive. I could sometimes catch glimpses of him at the end of a hallway, or retreating up the stairs as I came in the front door. And once, after dropping Vera off in the early morning, I came across Grisha out for a walk. He flared up suddenly in my headlights, his bandage a white ball on his narrow shoulders. It wasn't at all funny. It was as if I were seeing not Grisha but some terrible future, the future of my fears.

I made up my mind to live with Vera's moods, as I wanted to think of them, even while they grew more outrageous. I tried to see them as evidence of a rich, passionate nature. What other girl had ever cared enough about me to destroy my car? She'd even threatened to shoot herself once, pulling a pistol out of a desk drawer as I was about to leave her house in the middle of a quarrel. It was pure theater, I understood that, but a small doubt remained, and a small doubt was too much for me, so I gave in and stayed. I nearly always gave in. This became part of the trouble between us. Once she got her way she despised me for letting her have it, and immediately started pushing again. She had to find that line I wouldn't cross, where my cussedness was equal to hers. On this ground we fought like sworn enemies. We held nothing back, and once we were exhausted, after we'd given and taken every hurt, we came together with a tenderness that lasted for days, until the next round began. It was a hard way to be in love, and not the way I'd hoped for, but it was our way.

To be out of the barracks and the uniform. To be young and in love, surrounded by friends, free in a great city. To have my own time, to read, to loaf, to see plays, to hit jazz bars with Geoffrey and stay up until dawn talking about books and writing – all this was to forget for hours, even days at a time, that I had a bill coming due. But I found reasons to remember.

This was late '66, early '67. The news kept getting worse. More troops going over, more getting killed, some of them boys I'd known. I was afraid of the war, but I had never questioned its necessity. Among the soldiers I'd served with that question didn't even get raised. We took the official explanations on faith and did not ask for details. Faith carried no weight in Washington. My brother and most of my friends believed that the war was an atrocious mistake and ridiculed the government's attempts to justify it. I argued with them, furiously at times, but I didn't have command of the subject and my ignorance got me in trouble, never more than when I locked horns with I. F. Stone one night at Geoffrey's house. With exquisite gentleness, Stone peeled my bluster like an onion until there was nothing left but silence.

I began to attend Professor Carroll Quigley's Vietnam lectures at Georgetown. I went to a teach-in, but left after the first couple of speakers. They were operating out of their own faith system; faith in the sanctity of Ho Chi Minh and his cause, faith in the perfidy of those who were unconvinced. Mostly I read: Bernard Fall, Jules Roy, Lucien Bodard, Graham Greene.

The Quiet American affected me disagreeably. I liked to think that good intentions had value. In this book good intentions accomplished nothing but harm. Cynicism and accommodation appeared, by comparison, almost virtuous. I didn't like that idea. It seemed decadent, like the opium-addicted narrator and the weary atmosphere of the novel. What really bothered me was Greene's portrayal of Pyle, the earnest, blundering American. I did not fail to hear certain tones of my own voice in his, and this was irritating, even insulting. Yet I read the book again, and again.

In time I lost whatever certitudes I'd had, but I didn't replace them with new ones. The war was something I had to get through. Where was the profit in developing convictions that would make it even harder? I dabbled in unauthorized ideas, and at the point where they began to demand a response from me I drew back, closed my mind as if it were a floodgate, as if I could control the influx of doubt. But I was already up to my neck in it.

My mother lived within walking distance. We had dinner together at least once a week. She liked making a fuss over me, and I liked letting her do it. One night I was sitting in her living room while she cooked up some spaghetti. Her husband, Frank, was out somewhere. She moved around the kitchen, humming along to the radio – 101 Strings,

Mantovani. Easy listening. The apartment was warm and smelled good. She had filled it with mementos of her travels: Spanish dolls and Brazilian puppets, posters, goat-hair rugs, a camel saddle from Morocco, where she'd spent two weeks driving through the Atlas Mountains with a friend. I sat on the sofa with my legs crossed, drinking a beer and reading the newspaper. While I was in this state of contentment I saw Hugh Pierce's name among those of the dead.

It was no mistake. His name, rank, and unit were all there. I kept reading the words, and each time they floated farther away from my comprehension. I understood only one thing: This shouldn't have happened. It was wrong. I knew it at that moment as well as I know it now.

I called out to my mother. She came to the kitchen doorway and stood there looking at me. She was on guard, she knew something was up. I told her Hugh had been killed. I said it reproachfully; and my mother frowned and pushed her lips together like a girl who'd been scolded. Then she crossed the room and sat beside me and touched my wrist doubtfully. "Oh, Toby," she said.

I knew there was something I should do, but I didn't know what. I began to walk back and forth while my mother watched me. She told me to go on home if I wanted to be alone, we could have our dinner another time. But I discovered that I was hungry. Famished. I sat down and cleaned my plate and let my mother fill it again. I didn't talk and neither did she. Afterward I sat there and tried to form an intention. I couldn't think at all. I felt weightless. My hands were on the table as if I were about to push myself up decisively, but I stayed where I was. My mother looked on, stricken and afraid. For her sake I knew

66

I had to get out of there. I said maybe I'd better go home after all.

I didn't remember Yancy's letter until late that night. I got out of bed and opened the top drawer of the dresser, where I kept my correspondence and receipts. I riffled through the pile. She had loopy, girlish handwriting, and she'd used a pencil. I could recognize the envelope at a glance and often did, with a pang, when I was looking for something else. I knew it was there, but I didn't come up with it the first time through, nor the second.

I slid the drawer out and put it on the floor and knelt beside it. One by one I lifted every letter, turned it over, set it aside. When the drawer was empty I still hadn't found it. I was close to panic. I sat back and imposed calm on myself. The letter had to be somewhere in the room.

Taking care not to hurry, I searched the other drawers. I looked under the dresser, then pulled it away from the wall and looked behind it. I emptied my duffel bag, went through the pockets of my civvies and even my uniforms. I ran my hands over the shelves in the closet. When I heard myself panting I sat on the edge of my bed and forced myself to think back to when I'd last seen the letter. I couldn't. I got up again, took stock. Quietly, so I wouldn't wake the house, I began to tear my room to pieces. I left no inch of it unexamined. Nothing. Yancy's letter was gone. Had I thrown it away? Could I have done that – just thrown it away?

I couldn't even remember her last name.

A few days later I thought of calling her friend, the girl I'd taken out, but the number had been disconnected and her name wasn't listed in the directory. I called the bar where they'd both worked. No one knew any girls named Trace or Yancy.

I don't know exactly what I would have done if I'd found Yancy. Given her the news, of course. Tried to find out if she'd had the baby. I wanted to ask her about the baby – lots of questions there. And I would have said I was sorry for sitting on her letter, because I was sorry, I am still sorry, God knows I am sorry.

Vera and I fought more riotously every week. She took offense at something during a party and hewed out great clumps of her hair with pinking shears. One night she climbed the tree outside my bedroom window with a rope around her neck and threatened to hang herself. The outlandishness of our quarrels isolated us, and made reconciliation harder. We had to keep upping the ante, promising more of ourselves, to put the last one behind. Just before I finished language school we got engaged.

And then my year of grace ended. At the end of it, scared, short-winded, forgetful of all martial skills and disciplines, I was promoted to first lieutenant and posted back to Fort Bragg to await orders.

Just after I got there I was assigned to a training exercise being played out in the mountains of Pisgah National Forest. I didn't know any of the men whose temporary commander I became; I was filling in for their regular team leader, who had other business to attend to. Our job was to parachute in and link up with another team and make a show of our expertise.

It was over a year since I'd been in the field. In that time I had done almost no exercise, nor had I worn a uniform, carried a rifle and pack, or given an order. I hadn't read a compass or used a map except on drives into the countryside. On the day before the drop I locked myself up with plenty of coffee and every field manual I could get my hands on, like a student boning up for a chemistry final.

We gathered on the airstrip well before dawn. I tagged along with the first sergeant while he made the equipment check, looking on as if I knew what he was doing. It was still dark when we boarded the plane. I sat with the others until we entered the forest, then I hooked up my parachute and stood in the open doorway, trying to follow our position on the map. There was light breaking on the tops of the hills but the land below was still in darkness and the map kept flapping in my hand. Our pilot was supposed to flash a green warning light when he saw the smoke marking the drop zone, but I knew better than to rely on him. We were moving fast. If out of distraction or malice he was even a little slow giving us the signal we could end up in impossible terrain, miles from the drop zone and the men we were supposed to meet.

We were flying up a long valley. The slopes were awash in light, the plain was turning gray. We passed a cluster of houses. I tried to find the village on the map; it was unmarked, or I was looking in the wrong place. In fact I had no idea where we were. As the valley began to narrow, the plane descended and slowed. This was the usual prelude to the jump, but the green light still hadn't come on. I braced myself in the doorway and looked out. Smoke was rising off the valley floor a mile or so ahead of us. Our smoke was supposed to be yellow, and this was black, but it was the only smoke out there. I turned to the first sergeant. His eyes were closed. I looked back out the door and confirmed what I'd seen. Smoke. But still no green light.

A decision was required. It was my duty to make it. I gave the order to hook up, and as the first man came to the door I smacked him on the rump like a quarterback breaking the huddle and shouted "Go!" Then the next man, and the next, until everyone was out but me, and then I jumped.

Sudden silence. Mountains all around. The eerie, lovely sight of the other canopies, the men swinging below. My men. I'd gotten them out in good order, and with no help from the pilot. If I could manage this, I could manage the next thing. That was the secret – not to think ahead too much, not to rehearse every single step in advance. Just do what was needed as the need arose.

Then the man closest to the ground gave a shout and I looked down and saw him hauling like crazy on his risers, trying to change the path of his fall. The others started doing the same thing, and a moment later, when I got a good look at what lay below us, so did I.

We were not, as I had supposed, drifting down upon a field marked with signal grenades, but over the expanse of a vast garbage dump where random fires smoldered, sending greasy coils of smoke high into the air. I caught my first whiff a couple of hundred feet up and the smell got worse the closer I came. I pulled hard to the left, making for a patch of ground not yet covered with junk. I was lucky; being last out, I was fairly close to the edge. Almost everyone else landed in the soup. I watched them go down as I drifted to port, and listened to them bellow and swear, and heard the crunching sounds they made as they slammed into the dump.

We were several miles from the drop zone. To get there took us most of the day. No one spoke to me. It was as if I did not exist. We maintained this arrangement until our part in the exercise was over.

Two weeks later I was in Vietnam.

White Man

A week or so after Sergeant Benet and I made our Thanks-giving raid on Dong Tam, the division was ordered into the field. The plan called for our howitzers and men to be carried by helicopter to a position in the countryside. I was sent ahead with the security force responsible for preparing the ground and making sure it was safe to land. My job was to call in American gunships and medevacs if any were needed. I could even get F-14 Phantom jets if we ran into serious trouble, or trouble that I might consider serious, which would be any kind of trouble at all.

The designated position turned out to be a mud-field. We were ordered to secure another site some four or five kilometers away. Our march took us through a couple of deserted villages along a canal. This was a free-fire zone. The people who'd lived around here had been moved to a detention camp, and their home ground declared open to random shelling and bombing. Harassment and interdiction, it was called, H and I. The earth was churned up by artillery and pocked with huge, water-filled craters from B-52 strikes. Pieces of shrapnel, iridescent with heat scars, glittered underfoot. The dikes had been breached. The paddies were full of brackish water covered by green, undulant slime, broken here and there by clumps of saw grass. The silence was unnatural, expectant. It magnified the sound of our voices, the clank of mess kits and weapons, the rushing static of the radio. Our progress was not stealthy.

The villas were empty, the hooches in shreds, but you could see that people had been in the area. We kept coming across their garbage and cooking fires. Cooking fires – just like a Western. In the second village we found a white puppy. Someone had left him a heap of vegetable slops with some meat and bones mixed in. It looked rotten, but he seemed to be doing okay, the little chub. One of the soldiers tied a rope around his neck and brought him along.

Because the paddies were flooded and most of the dikes broken or collapsed, we had only a few possible routes of march, unless we moved off the trail; but mucking through the paddies was a drag, and our boys wouldn't dream of it. Though I knew better I didn't blame them. Instead we kept to what little remained of dry land, which meant a good chance of booby traps and maybe a sniper. There were several troops ahead of me in the column and I figured they'd either discover or get blown up by anything left on the trail, but the idea of a sniper had me on edge. I was the tallest man out here by at least a head, and I had to stay right next to the radio operator, who had this big squawking box on his back and a long antenna whipping back and forth over his helmet. And of course I was white. A perfect target. And that was how I saw myself, as a target, a long white face quartered by crosshairs.

I was dead sure somebody had me in his sights. I kept

scanning the tree lines for his position, feeling him track me. I adopted an erratic walk, slowing down and speeding up, ducking my head, weaving from side to side. We were in pretty loose order anyway so nobody seemed to notice except the radio operator, who watched me curiously at first and then went back to his own thoughts. I prepared a face for the sniper to judge, not a brave or confident face but not a fearful one either. What I tried to do was look well-meaning and slightly apologetic, like a very nice person who has been swept up by forces beyond his control and set down in a place where he knows he doesn't belong and that he intends to vacate the first chance he gets.

But at the same time I knew the sniper wouldn't notice any of that, would notice nothing but my size and my whiteness. I didn't fit here. I was out of proportion not only to the men around me but to everything else – the huts, the villages, even the fields. All was shaped and scaled to the people whose place this was. Time had made it so. I was oafish here, just as the Vietnamese seemed oddly dainty on the wide Frenchified boulevards of Saigon.

And man, was I white! I could feel my whiteness shooting out like sparks. This wasn't just paranoia, it was what the Vietnamese saw when they looked at me, as I had cause to know. One instance: I was coming out of a bar in My Tho some months back, about to head home for the night, when I found myself surrounded by a crowd of Vietnamese soldiers from another battalion. They pressed up close, yelling and pushing me back and forth. Some of them had bamboo sticks. They were mad about something but I couldn't figure out what, they were shouting too fast and all at once. *Tai sao?* I kept asking – Why? Why? I saw that the question infuriated them, as if I were denying some outrage that everyone there had personally seen me commit. I understood that this was a ridiculous misunderstanding, that they had me confused with another man, another American.

"I'm the wrong man," I said. "The wrong man!"

They became apoplectic. I couldn't get anywhere with them, and I soon wearied of trying. As I pushed my way toward the jeep one of them slashed me across the face with his stick and then the rest of them started swinging too, shoving for position, everyone trying to get his licks in. I fought back but couldn't hold them off. Because of my height I took most of the punishment on my shoulders and neck, but they managed to hit me a few more times in the face, not heavy blows but sharp and burning, as from a whip. Blood started running into my eyes. They were swinging and screaming, totally berserk, and then they stopped. There was no sound but the feral rasp and pant of our breathing. Everyone was looking at the bar, where an American lieutenant named Polk stood in the doorway. He was the one they were after, that was clear from his expression and from theirs.

With an unhurried movement Polk unsnapped his holster and took out his .45 and cocked it. He slowly aimed the pistol just above their heads, and in the same dream time they stepped back into the street and walked silently away.

Polk lowered the pistol. He asked if I was all right.

"I guess," I said. "What was that all about, anyway?"

He didn't tell me.

I was halfway home before it occurred to me that I could

have saved myself a lot of trouble by pulling my own pistol. I'd forgotten I had it on.

Sergeant Benet cleaned my wounds – a few shallow cuts on my forehead. He had a touch as gentle as a woman's, and feeling him take me so tenderly in hand, dabbing and clucking, wincing at my pain as if it were his own, I started to feel sorry for myself. "I don't get it," I said. "Polk doesn't look anything like me. He's almost as big as you are. He doesn't have a moustache. He's got these piggy little eyes and this big moon face. We don't look *anything* alike!"

"Why, you poor nigger," Sergeant Benet said. "You poor, poor nigger."

Which is all by way of saying that even as I composed my face for the sniper, making it shine forth my youth and good nature and hope for years to come, I had no illusion that he would see anything but its color.

We found the second position to be satisfactory and set up camp for the night. Though the troops weren't supposed to build fires, they did, as always. They dropped their weapons any old place and took off their boots and readied their pans for the fish they'd collected earlier that day by tossing hand grenades into the local ponds. While they cooked they called back and forth to each other and sang along with sad nasal ballads on their radios. The perimeter guards wouldn't stay in position; they kept drifting in to visit friends and check on the progress of the food.

Nights in the field were always bad for me. I had a case of the runs. My skin felt crawly. My right eye twitched, and I kept flinching uncontrollably. I plotted our coordinates and called them in to the firebase and the air support people, along with the coordinates of the surrounding tree lines and all possible avenues of attack. If we got hit I intended to call down destruction on everything around me – the whole world, if necessary. The puppy ran past, squealing like a pig, as two soldiers chased after him. He tumbled over himself and one of the troops jumped for him and caught him by a hind leg. He lifted him that way and gave him a nasty shake, the way you'd snap a towel, then walked off swinging the puppy's nose just above the ground. After I finished my calls I followed them over to one of the fires. They had tied the puppy to a tree. He was all curled in on himself, watching them with one wild eye. His sides were heaving.

I greeted the two soldiers and hunkered down at their fire. They were sitting face-to-face with their legs dovetailed, massaging each other's feet. The arrangement looked timeless and profoundly corporeal, like two horses standing back to front, whisking flies from one another's eyes. Seeing them this way, whipped and sore, mired in their bodies, emptied me of anger. I shared my cigarettes. We agreed that Marlboros were number one.

I motioned toward the dog. "What are you going to call him?"

They looked at me without understanding.

"The dog," I said. "What name are you going to give him?"

The younger of the two gave a snort. The other, a sergeant with gray hair, stared at the puppy and said, "Canh Cho. His name is Canh Cho."

Dog Stew.

The one who had snorted lay back and shrieked like a

girl being tickled, banging his knees together. Some other soldiers wandered over to see what was happening.

I addressed myself to the sergeant. He had a thin, scholarly face and a grave manner. When he spoke to me he lowered his head and looked up from under his eyebrows. I said, "Are you really going to eat him?"

"Oh yes." He smacked his lips and made greedy spooning gestures. Then he turned to the newcomers and repeated our conversation. They laughed. Gold teeth flashed in the firelight.

"When are you going to eat him?"

"Oh, tonight."

"Tonight? He's pretty small, isn't he? Don't you want to wait until he's bigger?"

"No," the sergeant said. "Now is the best time. The meat is best now." He made the spooning motions again. He said, "Let's eat!" and stood and untied the puppy, then picked him up by the tail and carried him to the fire. Looking at his friends and dancing a clownish jig, he dangled the yelping little wretch over the flames.

"Don't do that," I said, and everything changed, or became clear. I saw it in the sergeant's face, felt it in the hardening silence of the others. Up to now we'd been a couple of soldiers messing around in a soldierly way. But I had drawn a line, or at least called attention to the line already between us. I had spoken in absolute confidence of my mastery here. Now he had no choice but to show me – I could feel it coming – his own view of the situation.

The sergeant pulled the pup away from the fire and studied me. Then he hung it over the fire again. It gagged in the smoke and raked the air with its paws.

"Stop it!" I said, and got up.

He moved the puppy back long enough to let it catch its breath, then swung it like a censer back and forth through the flames. All this time his eyes were on me. I knew I should keep my mouth shut, but when the pup started choking I couldn't help myself. I ordered him to stop. Again he pulled the pup back, again he held it to the fire, again I told him to stop. And again. He wasn't playing with the dog, he was playing with me, with my whiteness, my Americanness, my delicate sentiments — everything that gave me my sense of superior elevation. And I knew it. But knowing did not free me from these conditions, it only made me feel how hopelessly subject I was to them.

Please, what was I doing here? If I'd been forced to say what I was doing out here in this alien swamp, forced to watch an ignorant man oppress a dog, could I, with a straight face, have said, "I am an adviser"?

I couldn't win. My only choice was to quit. I turned and walked away, until I heard a howl of such despair that I had to stop. It seemed I didn't have a choice after all. Nor did the sergeant, grimly waiting for me with the singed and gasping pup. He was locked in the game too, as much as I was. He had to take it to the end.

I could think of only one way out. I said, as if this had been the question all along, "All right. How much?"

The sergeant was no dope; he saw his opening. He looked at the puppy. "A thousand piastres," he said.

"A thousand piastres? Too much. Five hundred."

"A thousand."

I made an aggrieved face but got out my wallet and paid

him. It didn't kill me – five dollars and change. He took the money and gave me the smoking dog. The other soldiers had been stern and watchful, holding him to his task, but now they were joking around again. They were satisfied. Profit was victory.

"Good-bye, Canh Cho," one of them called.

I took the puppy back to my tent. His fur was scorched and greasy with soot, his eyes bloodshot, his nose blistered. He smelled like rancid bacon. I cleaned him up as well as I could and tried to calm him. He trembled convulsively. Every time I touched him he yipped in fright and shrank away. I spoke to him in low, gentle tones and when he continued to cringe I began to dislike him. I disliked him for being so unlucky. I disliked him for involving me in his bad luck, and making a fool of me. I disliked him for not seeing any difference between me and the man who'd hurt him.

But I held him and petted him and finally he fell asleep in my lap, his nose tucked between my knees. While he slept I went on stroking him, and my hands grew slow and gentle with the memory of all the other dogs they'd known, Sheppy and Tyke, Ringer, Banana, Champion, and without warning tenderness overcame me. It spread through me like a blush, like the sudden heat of unexpected praise – an exotic sensation, almost embarrassing in its intensity. I hardly recognized it. I hadn't felt anything like it in months.

The radio operator brought me a plate of rice and fish. He looked at the pup and made the same eating gesture the sergeant had made. He rubbed his stomach and laughed, and walked away laughing.

•   •   •

From that day on it became the custom of our troops to greet me with spooning motions and signs of ravenous appetite, especially when I took Canh Cho out for a walk. He seemed to understand their meaning. He was a sad little pooch. I tried to teach him a few tricks, bring out some personality, make a proper mascot of him so he'd have a place in the battalion after I was gone. Nothing doing. He wouldn't even chase a ball unless I smeared hamburger on it. All he wanted to do was lie under the big wicker chair with his head sticking out and snap at flies. This engaged his interest, and he was certainly good at it, but it seemed a raw, unfriendly sort of pleasure.

Shortly after Christmas Vera wrote to tell me she'd been seeing someone else, "seriously." She thought it best to suspend our engagement until things were clearer. I read the letter many times over, not sure how to respond. Though I managed to strike a note of offended trust and virtue in my letter back to Vera, I didn't really feel it, and knew I had no right to it. The truth was, I'd been unfaithful to her ever since I got to My Tho. I made resolutions, and renewed them now and then, but they never survived any temptation worth the name. Nor had I given Vera much to hang on to. My letters home were by turns casual and melodramatic, and had little to say of love. If, as she'd asked me to do, I had written truthfully about my inner life, I would have written about boredom, dread, occasional outright fear, and the sexual hunger that fear left boiling in its wake.

Still, Vera's letter gave me a knock. It caused me to compare myself to the other fellow, Leland. We had never met, but I'd heard Vera speak of him as an old friend.

Though only a year my senior, Leland was a college graduate with a good job. She had once said that he was brilliant. The word went down hard even then, as if I'd sensed how it would come back to judge me later.

Using Leland's blazing sun to take my bearings, I looked around and found myself exactly nowhere. No marketable education, no money, no prospects. My writing, my "work" as I'd begun to call it, was supposed to take care of all that. Mindful of the feckless dropout Scott Fitzgerald leaving the army with a finished draft of *This Side of Paradise* in his duffel bag, about to feed lifelong dust to his classmates, I had promised myself that I would use my nights to finish the novel I'd begun in Washington; but it soon came to seem romantic and untrue, and I conceived an implacable hatred for it.

Probably it was romantic. Most first novels are. As to whether it was untrue, that's another question. I believed in it when I first started writing it, believed in its story and the view of things that held it together. The truth of a novel proceeds from just that kind of conviction, carried to extremes. I had it, then I didn't. The ground shifted under my feet; the old view vanished and of the one still taking shape I could make neither poetry nor sense. I put the novel out of sight. Eventually, ceremonially, I burned it.

I was unable to write anything else. Instead I tried to read the books Geoffrey took such pains to choose and send me, but over the past several months my passion for them had gone flat as well. It became a duty to read each sentence, and the books themselves felt awkward and foreign in my hands. Before long I'd catch myself staring off. This was my signal to join Sergeant Benet for *Bonanza* or *The Gong Show*, or brave the road for a run into town. The best thing I had to say for myself was that I was still alive. Not impressively, though. Not brilliantly.

Strange, how the memory of that one word – she didn't use it in the letter – could give me so stark a picture of my condition. Even more than the letter itself, even more than losing Vera, whose loss, to tell the truth, did not seem impossible to bear, that word cast me down. I called Canh Cho over, thinking it would be agreeable to have him lay his head on my knee and look up at me while I stroked him and pondered my state. But he didn't move.

"Come here, damn you."

He pulled his head back under the chair.

I stood and lifted the chair to show him he couldn't hide from me, anywhere. He looked up and understood, then lowered his head in the woe of his knowledge. I put the chair back down. I was sorry, but what a sad dog. I had to conclude that he probably would have been happier with the Vietcong, unless, of course, they ate him.

Close Calls

I was inclined to regard every day I got through alive as a close call. I knew I could be killed at any moment, in any number of ways, randomly in the general mayhem or at the particular wish of the Vietcong who were everywhere around us. I wasn't hard to keep track of; they must have known my comings and goings. To kill me would have been easy, a piece of cake, and that they hadn't bothered to do it showed a just appreciation of my importance to the war effort. I was alive because they didn't consider me worth killing. I understood that, perfectly. I also understood that they might change their minds, take it into their heads that I mattered somehow. Who could guess their reasons? Their reasons were their own. I felt myself hanging by a thread in some boss guerrilla's mind, subject to his mood swings, his insomnia, his desperation to be taken seriously by other guerrillas. So while it might have been fainthearted of me to picture the days ahead as a long minefield, and the days behind as a series of reprieves, it was also perfectly accurate. But that's not what we mean by a close call.

I had been shot at. More accurately, shots had been fired in my direction from afar, without effect on me or the men I was with. Mortars had fallen in my neighborhood – none of them very close. I'd traveled in convoys where other men got blown up by mines and been in a helicopter that got hit, but not punctured, by machine gun fire (Sergeant Benet and I felt the bullets pounding against the metal under our feet, and gaped at each other in naked horror as our door gunner giggled and blasted away with his own machine gun).

None of these were close calls. A close call is personal, mysterious, sometimes fantastic. A bullet enters a man's helmet center-front and exits center-rear without putting a scratch on him. A platoon gets ambushed and overrun, after which the enemy puts a round in every man's head save one. A medic falls unnoticed from a pitching helicopter a thousand yards up and lands feetfirst in a rice paddy, plunging to his neck in the mud, where an American patrol rescues him, entirely by accident, the next morning. Things like this happened every day, and the best stories got written up in *Stars and Stripes* with a picture of the lucky guy. My own close calls were pretty thin gruel by comparison but good enough for me. Up until Tet I'd had two or three, depending on whether you counted the last.

My first close call happened a few days after I joined the battalion. I'd just had time to get unpacked and draw battle gear from the quartermaster when we got orders for the field. The operation took place over Easter weekend. Our guns were set up near a Catholic church, one of the few I ever saw in the Delta. On Sunday morning I woke to the sound of tolling bells, and later, as I sat hunched over my coffee, I was smitten by the sight of laughing girls in white ao dais leaping like lambs across the muddy furrows behind our howitzers. Though I had seldom been to mass since I was a boy, I accepted Sergeant Benet's invitation to join him.

The service was in Latin. The sound of the old tongue, the smell of incense, the once-familiar rhythm of the liturgy gave me a sense of continuity with my own past, as if this place were not wholly different from other places I had been. I didn't take communion, but I was pleased at how unhesitatingly I stood and knelt with the others, how quickly the responses came to my lips. I was glad to have Sergeant Benet there beside me. Up to now I'd been unsure of him, afraid he'd despise me for my fumbling inexperience, my incomprehensible officer status. But seeing him bow his head and pray for leniency gave me hope for some from him. When he said "Pax Christi, sir" and held out his hand, I took it with gratitude. Then I bowed to the Vietnamese around me as they were bowing to one another.

Without marking the change in myself, I had begun to let go a little, lulled from the state of paranoid watchfulness I'd been in since my first night off the plane. A mistake. Fear won't always save you, but it will take some of the pressure off your luck.

After mass Sergeant Benet and I drove to the village market to buy some fresh bread and vegetables. While he did the shopping I leaned back in the passenger seat and closed my eyes. My mood was still churchy, sentimental, liquid. I hadn't slept much the night before, and now, surrounded by friendly indecipherable voices and warmed by the sun, I began to nod off. Then I became aware that the voices had stopped. The silence disturbed me. I sat up and looked around. The crowd had drawn back in a wide circle. They were staring at me. A woman yammered something I couldn't follow and pointed under the jeep. I bent down for a look. There, lying directly below my seat, was a hand grenade. The pin had been pulled. I straightened up and sat there for a while, barely breathing. Then I got out of the jeep and walked over to where everyone else was standing. We were still within the grenade's killing range, especially if it set off the gas tank, but I didn't think of that any more than the others had. I didn't have a thought in my head. We just stood there like a bunch of fools.

Sergeant Benet appeared at the edge of the crowd. "What's going on?" he said.

"There's a grenade under the jeep."

He turned and looked. "Oh, man," he said. He dropped the groceries and started pushing people back, his arms outstretched like a riot cop's. "*Di di mau!*" he kept saying. "Beat it! Beat it!" Finally they gave ground, except for a bunch of kids who surrounded him and refused to be driven off. They were laughing. I looked on. None of it seemed to have anything to do with me.

Once the area was cleared Sergeant Benet told a couple of skittish villagers to stand watch until we could send someone to take care of the grenade; then we started walking back to the battalion. Along the way I found my legs acting funny. My knees wouldn't lock; I had to lean against a wall. Sergeant Benet put his hand on my arm to steady me. Then something went slack in my belly and I felt a stream of shit pouring hotly out of me, down my legs, even into my boots. I put my head against the wall and wept for very shame.

"It's all right, sir," Sergeant Benet said. "You'll be all right." He patted me on the back. Then he said, "Come on, sir. You got yourself a little case of the turistas, that's all. Here, that's the way. Just a step at a time, sir, that's right. Easy does it."

The grenade never did go off on its own. Our ordnance disposal boys covered it with sandbags and triggered it with a dose of plastique. It was an American grenade, not some local mad bomber device. The odds of it failing like that were cruelly small — just about nonexistent, in fact.

That was my first close call.

My second close call was of a more civilian character, the kind of thing that happens on road crews and construction sites. Still, it almost nailed me.

I'd been with the battalion for about six months. One of my jobs was to hook up our howitzers to Chinook helicopters when they were needed elsewhere in a hurry or when we were about to be inserted into an area we couldn't reach by road. I would rig up the gun in a sling, then stand on top of it as the chopper slowly lowered itself toward me, flattening the grass, raising a storm of dust and dirt and paddy water against which I wore ski goggles I'd asked Vera to send me. When the Chinook was a couple of feet over my head, just hanging there, all lebenty zillion tons of it, I would raise a steel loop and work it onto the hook dangling from the bottom of the helicopter. Then I'd nod at the crew chief and the cables would tighten and creak and I'd jump down and the chopper would lift the howitzer straight up, then cumbersomely bank and turn and beat a slanting path slowly higher and away into the distance. You saw all kinds of things swinging under those monster helicopters: howitzers, trucks, other helicopters; even, after a fight somewhere, nets filled with body bags.

My big fear was that a Chinook would lurch down and crush me against the gun. This could easily happen. All it took was for one of the engines to miss, or the pilot to sneeze, or a sudden downdraft to hit the rotors. I was always on the scout for any sign of unsteadiness – not that I would have had time to do anything. But once the cables went taut I was free to jump, and jump I did, without decorum. While the helicopter maneuvered overhead I brushed myself off and gathered up the sling they'd tossed down for the next pickup.

In the early days I used to watch as the Chinook hauled its load into the sky; it was a strange sight, but I got used to it and had other things to attend to. I don't know what made me look up this one time. Maybe I heard a new sound under the engine clatter and the whapping of the blades, a sound I didn't even know I was hearing, a different sound than what my self-loving body had recorded as acceptable to its interests. Anyway, I looked up sharply. The Chinook was directly above me, sixty, seventy feet, executing an elephantine turn. The howitzer was swinging back and forth. From this vantage I could see nothing wrong, but even so I started to walk backward off the LZ, my eyes raised, and I saw the howitzer shift oddly in its sling, and shift again, and then the sling flew open and the chopper jumped like a flea. The howitzer seemed to fall very slowly, turning as it fell, and landed upside down with a painful blaring whang – more a sensation than a sound – and bounced once and settled. I felt the shock from my heels to my teeth.

This would not be a proper close call story if I didn't point out that the gun hit right where I'd been standing.

The third close call happened just before Christmas. I didn't mention it to anyone afterward, unlike the other two, which I talked about every chance I got. This one didn't really sound all that dangerous and it wouldn't have made a satisfactory story. Still; I brooded on it more than on the others.

We were on an operation. Sergeant Benet stayed with the battalion while I pulled duty at the fire direction center. On the second day, one of our infantry companies walked into an ambush. I was hanging around the headquarters tent at the time, idly listening to situation reports come in over the radio, and I heard the battle begin and the Vietnamese commander cry through the static for help.

General Ngoc took over from the radio operator. His staff officers crowded around to listen. There was plenty to hear. Screams. Gunfire. The voices of men in terror and pain. Colonel Lance, the ranking American adviser, came over to the radio, puffing fiercely on his pipe as he watched General Ngoc bark into the transmitter at the frightened commander in the field. Colonel Lance didn't speak Vietnamese but he narrowed his eyes and nodded from time to time as if he knew what was passing between the two men. And as he stood there listening he absently laid one hand on the shoulder of the officer standing next to him, a first lieutenant named Keith Young. He didn't look to see who it was; he just rested his hand on him the way a football coach will rest his hand on the player he happens to be standing next to on the sidelines. It was one of those paternal gestures that excited my scorn except when they fell on me, and then I always felt a flood of puppyish gratitude.

Anyway, Colonel Lance didn't look to see who was there when he parked his hand. It could have been anyone. It could have been me. It could very easily have been me, as I was standing beside Keith Young at the time, and if Colonel Lance had taken a place between us instead of to Keith's right it would have been me who got the manly sign of favor. He stood there with his hand on Keith's shoulder, and when General Ngoc got up from the radio and explained the situation, which was that the company was pinned down and taking casualties, and needed an American adviser to go in with the reinforcements to call in medevacs and air support, Colonel Lance turned to the man he had his hand on and looked him in the face for the first time. He took his pipe out of his mouth. "Well, Keith," he said, "what do you think?" His voice was kind, his expression solicitous. If you didn't know better you'd have thought he was asking an opinion, not giving an order, but Keith did know better. "I'll get my stuff," he said. His voice was flat. He looked at me as he walked past.

Colonel Lance nodded at General Ngoc and reached for the transmitter. While he was calling for helicopters to insert the reserve company into the field I faded back and left the tent. Colonel Lance had taken no notice of me, and it seemed wise to keep it that way.

Keith got killed later that afternoon. I never heard what the circumstances were, only that he was shot in the stomach. That meant he'd been standing up, maybe to carry one end of a stretcher, or with his arm raised to give the textbook signal for attack – "Follow me!"

His death affected me strangely. It didn't cause me pain so much as a kind of wonder at the way it had happened. I couldn't stop playing it out: Colonel Lance hearing the fuss at the radio and walking over to see what was wrong, intent on the terrible sounds filling the air, heedless of either Keith or me except as big American bodies among the Vietnamese gathered around the table. Then his arbitrary decision to stand to Keith's right, no nearer the radio than if he'd stood between us. This was the decision from which everything else followed: the hand on Keith's shoulder, the gaze that followed the hand, the order that followed the gaze, the death that followed the order. Everything marched in lockstep from that one moment. If he had stood between us it would have been my shoulder the hand fell on, the other hand being occupied with his curved, fragrant, fatherly pipe. It would have been me receiving the father's thoughtless blessing touch, me to whom he turned, me to whom he put the kindly question that had only one answer.

It could have been me. I knew it even then, and Keith might have had the same thought. We were the same rank, had about the same experience. We both stood about six feet. He was older by two or three years, but not so you'd notice. For the needs of this occasion either of us seemed about as plausible as the other. He had grounds for wondering why the hand had fallen on him. It could have been me, and he may even have thought that it should have been me. Certainly there were times, not immediately afterward but in the months and years to come, that I myself

92

had the suspicion it should have been me – that Keith, and Hugh, and other men had somehow picked up my cards and stood in the place where I was meant to stand.

I once confessed this dreary notion to someone, who, meaning well, told me it was caveman talk.

"I know," I said. "But still."

But still. In a world where the most consequential things happen by chance, or from unfathomable causes, you don't look to reason for help. You consort with mysteries. You encourage yourself with charms, omens, rites of propitiation. Without your knowledge or permission the bottom-line caveman belief in blood sacrifice, one life buying another, begins to steal into your bones. How could it not? All around you people are killed: soldiers on both sides, farmers, teachers, mothers, fathers, schoolgirls, nurses, your friends – but not you. They have been killed instead of you. This observation is unavoidable. So, in time, is the corollary, implicit in the word *instead*: in place of. They have been killed in place of you – in your place. You don't think it out, not at the time, not in those terms, but you can't help but feel it, and go on feeling it. It's the close call you have to keep escaping from, the unending doubt that you have a right to your own life. It's the corruption suffered by everyone who lives on, that henceforth they must wonder at the reason, and probe its justice.

I didn't really know Keith Young. We saw each other in My Tho now and then, exchanged a few friendly words, but we didn't take it any farther than that. He was too quiet for me, too careful. He struck me, I have to admit, as a company man, and it was pretty clear that I'd made no better impression on him. We never spent any time

93

together until by chance we ran into each other while boarding the Kowloon ferry in Hong Kong. I'd been on R and R for four or five days already and Keith had just arrived. He was on his way to a tailor he'd heard about, and invited me to join him. This tailor was incredible, he said. For thirty dollars he could copy any suit; all you had to do was show him a picture of it. Keith had several pictures, advertisements he'd cut out of *Esquire*. You could pick up the suits in twenty-four hours.

I didn't have anything better to do so I went along with Keith and watched him being fitted for his wardrobe. At first I found the whole thing comical, especially a sign in the window of the shop: "Guaranteed by the Royal Navy." I liked the idea of the Royal Navy taking an interest in my duds. And then I began to think it wasn't that bad a deal, thirty bucks, and that it wouldn't hurt to have a few good suits and the odd sport coat hanging around. Before leaving the shop that day I placed some orders of my own, for clothes that did not in fact resemble the ones in *Esquire* – "You look like a Chinaman," a friend told me when I got home – and which quickly began to fall apart because of inferior thread. One of my suit sleeves actually came off inside my overcoat as I was arriving at a house for a dinner party some years later. I considered sending a letter of complaint to the First Lord of the Admiralty, but never did.

My haul was modest compared to Keith's. He ordered six or seven suits, tweed jackets, camel and blue blazers, slacks, button-down shirts of every acceptable color, formal wear, and two overcoats – also in camel and blue. He seemed bent on getting the whole clothes problem out of the way forever, right then and there. We hit a few clubs that night and he couldn't stop talking about what a great deal he'd gotten. And that was the first thought I had when I heard he'd been killed: What about all those clothes? It was a gasp of a thought, completely instinctual, without malice or irony. All those clothes waiting for him – they seemed somehow an irrefutable argument for his survival. Maybe they'd seemed that way to him too, a kind of guarantee, like the wives and fiancées some of us accumulated just before leaving home. They gave us a picture of ourselves in time to come, a promise of future existence to use as a safe-conduct pass through the present.

I sometimes tried to imagine other men wearing Keith's suits, but I couldn't bring the images to life. What I see instead is a dark closet with all his clothes hanging in a row. Someone opens the closet door, looks at them for a time, and closes the door again.

Duty

One of the local medical volunteers was a sour, livid Canadian named Macleod. He was full of absurd Scottish affectations that nobody had the nerve to call him on because his tongue was so sharp. Doc Macleod believed that at all times and in all places he was surrounded by fools. I never saw him laugh. Once in a blue moon, when hilarity got the better of him, he'd point his finger and say, "Funny." Doc Macleod had joined a church-sponsored medical team bound for Vietnam right after his residency in Toronto, because he planned to be a surgeon and thought that the misery here would give him a great chance to perform operations.

"Laddy," he told me, "without war we'd still be swinging in the fucking trees. It's God's own university and anyone who says different is a self-deluding fairy."

Doc Macleod looked on me as a fool in the making, starved for instruction that I was too far gone in folly to profit by but which it was his thankless duty to provide. In this spirit he sometimes took me along when he paid his calls on militia outposts in the backwaters of the province.

These were mostly villages, never meant to serve as forts, that had the bad luck to be close to roads and rivers and canals. From these villages, the theory went, a communist-hating peasantry could maul the Vietcong as they moved through the area. It didn't work out that way. These people weren't belligerent mountain tribesmen or Nung mercenaries; they were farmers, and after they got home from training camp they took off their boots and tried to stay out of trouble. Their villages were easy prey. The Vietcong regularly attacked them to pick up weapons and show their strength.

I was under no obligation to go along on these trips, Medcaps as they were called, but they made me feel useful. That was why I kept going out. It was like being a missionary; even a god. A couple of us big white guys would drop out of the sky and spend the day surrounded by astonished rustics who fully expected us to perform miracles. Some of what they lined up to show us – blisters, boils, pyorrhea – Doc Macleod had me treat with first aid. He took care of the rest. The work kept me busy for a few hours, and did no harm. It wasn't even very dangerous; we descended in broad daylight and left before nightfall.

In one of these outposts I met an American sergeant named Fisher. He had been stationed there with a lieutenant who'd gotten killed a couple weeks back. Now Fisher was on his own until the lieutenant's replacement arrived. And what a place to be alone in. Every wall had holes in it. Most of the stucco had been blasted off the cinder-block community hall that Fisher and his lieutenant had helped build when they first arrived. The earthen wall around the perimeter still hadn't been properly filled in where mortar fire had blown gaps in it.

Fisher was young, twenty or twenty-one, and with his

jungle hat on he looked even younger. His skin was completely smooth. But when he took his hat off he aged fifty years. His hair was white. Not silver, not the lustrous thatch of the hale, deep-sleeping burgher, but dry wispy white. It was the hair of a used-up old man.

He blinked constantly. His voice was high and he talked a blue streak, stammering often. That was when he spoke to Doc Macleod and me. When he spoke to the Vietnamese he sounded calm and sure of himself. In the village there was a young child, a girl, with a cleft palate. Doc Macleod wanted to take her back with us and send her on to Saigon for corrective surgery. The mother went into hysterics. I tried to explain that she could go along with her daughter and stay with her in the hospital, but she refused to listen. Fisher went over to Doc Macleod and asked how important the operation was.

"She'll never get laid without it."

"Being beautiful isn't all that important here."

"She'll look like a fucking crocodile. Is that ugly enough for you?"

Fisher put his arm around the woman and walked her outside. I could hear how serenely he reasoned with her. She simply couldn't argue, Fisher was so quiet and certain of her submission. She went away and came back with a bundle and sat with her daughter until it was time to go.

After we finished up, Fisher invited me back to his quarters to wait for the helicopter. He and his lieutenant had fashioned a room for themselves in the back of the hall by hanging blankets on a rod. Fisher pulled them together to give us some privacy and offered me one of the Cokes we'd brought him, which I tried to refuse because I didn't want to deplete his store. He insisted. I took it and sat on the lieutenant's bunk and let Fisher bend my ear. Some kids gathered at the open window and watched us. They didn't say anything. A few of them had had their heads shaved that morning for parasites and were possibly worried about the consequences of drawing our attention again. Behind them I could see long strings of pig guts hanging between two poles; they were covered with flies whose furious buzzing never left my ears.

Fisher was telling me about the lieutenant who'd been killed. He was, by coincidence, from the same part of Illinois as Fisher himself, and their fathers were both high school teachers. They had become close friends in their isolation here. Fisher told me that he was in touch with the lieutenant's parents, that his own parents had driven over to see them and share the letters Fisher had written before the lieutenant got killed, in which he described his friend's courage and devotion to the villagers.

"Man, did he love these people," Fisher said. "You should've heard him speak the language. It was unbelievable."

"You're doing pretty well yourself."

"Not like him."

"How did he get killed?"

Fisher was sitting on the other bunk. He shook his head and stared at the dirt floor between his feet. "Not like him. He really worked at it. Wherever he went he was always pointing at stuff and saying, What's that? What's that? He was a Christian, you know? Everyone was family to him, everyone, that's just the kind of person he was."

"What happened to him?"

Fisher examined me as if trying to remember what I was doing there. "You a believer, sir?"

"I don't know. Sometimes. Sometimes not."

"I used to be. I'm not so sure, anymore. It doesn't make a whole lot of sense, when you really think about it. Like resurrection of the body, what're they going to do if you get blown up – find every little part of you and stick it all back together? What if part of you is in one country and the rest of you is in some other country?"

I heard the helicopter coming in. Fisher ignored the sound and kept talking.

"When you actually see what bodies are made of, you know, inside, it's kind of hard to think of all that stuff coming back together again ten thousand years later or whenever. I mean, how do they keep track? When you think of all the people that have died . . . that's a lot of people. The other thing is, how do they figure out who gets resurrected? If you're a saint or something, okay, sure, that's easy, but what if you're a Christian but you've killed people?"

Hesitantly, unsure of my right to speak on this subject, I said that God must understand how things like that happened. Fisher didn't seem to hear. He kept talking.

Doc Macleod called out from the other end of the hall. It was time to leave.

Fisher walked with me toward the field where the helicopter was waiting. His words came faster and faster, as if to weave a net of sound by which to snare me and hold me there. He was like a safecracker madly spinning the dials as the clock runs out on him. I stopped and said, "Why don't you come back with us?"

He didn't answer.

"Just get on and go," I said.

"I can't," he said, but I could see that he was thinking about it.

Doc Macleod was ahead of us, handing up the little girl to the crew chief. Her mother waited beside him, along with an older man who wore a chin beard. He was lean and bony. Ropy veins stood out on his neck and forearms.

"I'm not sure about this," Fisher said.

I didn't say anything. Now that I'd made the offer there was no taking it back, and who wouldn't want to see him safely out of this place? But I was also beginning to understand that people were going to be *beaucoup* unhappy with me if Sergeant Fisher deserted his post at my invitation. I couldn't begin to imagine where my troubles would end if he got on that helicopter.

It never came to that. While we were still at the edge of the field, some sort of dispute arose between the little girl's mother and the bearded man. He'd been holding her bundle and now he would not let go. He didn't jerk at it or try to wrestle it away from her, nor did he utter a sound, but he would not surrender it. She was weeping, quietly, without display. Fisher went up to them and spoke to the man, who let go and stepped back with Fisher and watched as Doc Macleod helped the woman up and then climbed on board himself. I followed him and buckled myself in and waved to Fisher. He didn't see me. He was busy making assurances, giving hope with his calm voice and the fact of his abiding presence. Duty had swallowed him whole, loneliness, fear, and all. His path was absolutely clear. I almost envied him.

Fisher looked up with the others but made no sign as the chopper lifted slowly off the field and climbed above the rooftops. The pilot passed over the village with a lumbering restraint that might have been courtesy, until we were clear of the perimeter. Then he hit the gas.

Doc Macleod and I went into My Tho for some fish soup that evening. As we drove in from the airfield it started to mist up and by the time we finished eating rain was falling in sheets and the sky was black. The hot soup, together with the rain pounding on the roof, made me heavy-limbed and thoughtful. I stared out the window while Doc Macleod worked on a model plane he'd produced from his bag. He always had a model going; he said it kept his hands steady. A column of Vietnamese soldiers walked down the street, rifles slung upside down beneath their glistening ponchos.

I said, "I wonder what made his hair turn white like that?"

"What unbearable experience, you mean? What terror too great for mortal man?"

"Something turned his hair white."

"I'll give you the short answer, laddy. That's the one you'll think you understand. Genes."

"I know that's the usual explanation."

"The only explanation, boyo."

"The only scientific explanation, you mean."

"Don't be a silly cunt."

"There are cases."

He put down the model. "You can't be serious."

"There are."

"Christ!" He threw himself back hard against the chair

and looked around at the waiter as if to call him as a witness to my stupidity.

"I know of one personally."

"Oh you do, do you? You didn't see it happen, did you? No. How curious. Every mother's son *personally* knows of a case, and nobody has seen it happen. You know what I fucking hate?" He leaned toward me. "More than anything else, sonny, I hate the condescension of ignorant sissies with all their *more things in heaven and earth Horatio* bullshit. It's too much to bear. You want a mystical explanation? Call it fate. Say, 'It was written.' That would be the whole bloody truth."

"It happened to someone in my ex fiancée's family. Not an actual family member – "

"Don't!" He put his hands over his ears.

This conversation passed from my mind until just after Tet, when I was searching through one of the makeshift hospitals in My Tho for some people who had disappeared without trace. I was dull from the smell of carbolic and sepsis and from the sight of all these bereft, mutely suffering people with their terrible wounds and lopped limbs. It was odd to feel the wholeness of my body as I made my way among them. And then I saw Doc Macleod across the room, walking regally between a row of cots. He saw me at the same time and stopped short. "My God, man," he said. "Your hair! It's white as snow!" He caught me completely flat-footed, and before I could stop myself I felt my hand fluttering toward my head. He smiled and shook his finger at me and moved off down the aisle, trailed by a fussing retinue of Vietnamese doctors and nurses. He was in his glory.

A Federal Offense

Just before Tet my father sent me a belated Christmas card in which he said he watched the Vietnam news every day and was "damned proud" of me. I knew he meant well, but I couldn't help wondering what he had in mind. What did he think I was doing over here? What would he like me to be doing? Something "hush-hush," maybe, something understatedly brave and important as in the stories he used to tell, or imply, about flying with the RAF and serving with partisans just about everywhere. But maybe not. In fact I didn't know what he expected from me, or what to expect from him.

He had gotten out of prison a couple of years back while I was in Officer Candidate School. A friend of his from the old days found him an apartment in Manhattan Beach, and my father wrote me from there to send news of his release and simply to wish me well. There was no humbug in the letter, no talk of impending deals or bum raps. He said Geoffrey was helping him out every month and that was how he'd gotten my address. Years had passed since I'd heard from him or made any effort of my own to get in touch, and I was astounded to see his broad, outsized scrawl, the letters almost like ideograms, on the envelope. I sent back my own good wishes and thereafter we exchanged notes every six months or so.

When I was in language school my father wrote to propose that he come to Washington for a grand reunion. He could catch up with his boys, meet Priscilla and Vera, and pay his respects to our mother (he had either forgotten, or didn't care, that she had married again). He saw no reason, if he found Washington to his liking, why something couldn't be worked out with his parole board that would allow him to move there.

Geoffrey and I had a talk about it. His sense of humor was not on display. To him, the idea of the old man in Washington was a pit filled with man-eating possibilities. I could see his point. For once in his life he was solvent and in place, even, as book editor of the *Washington Post*, something of a personage in town, a favored ambassador from the trivial but charming realm of literature. Priscilla was expecting their first child in a few months.

Enter the old man. It was obvious to both of us how the play would go, we knew the script by heart: exotic cars paid for with rubber checks, stereos and Dunhill lighters charged to "my boy over at the *Post*." Landlords, grocers, clothiers, purveyors of wine and spirits, loan sharks, all clamoring for justice – to Geoffrey. The whole thing would fall on him. It was unthinkable. But Geoffrey had thought about it; that was what made it hard for him. He had a lingering dream of somehow bringing the old man back into the family, and would have done just about anything to pull it off except let him destroy his life.

We declined our father's offer to join us, and he took it like a sport – nothing ventured, nothing gained – and said no more about it. But I'd gotten interested in seeing him again, and after my orders for Vietnam came in I arranged to take a quick detour to Manhattan Beach.

It started badly. When I got to LAX I couldn't find the envelope with his address. He was not allowed to have a phone – Ma Bell couldn't afford him. I tried calling Geoffrey, and got no answer. Then I remembered that a few months back there'd been a flap over some slippers and a tobacco pouch my father had charged at a Scandinavian imports store and neglected to pay for. He'd almost gone back to prison on account of it, but Geoffrey made good for him and the owner dropped charges. The name of the store had stayed with me. I looked it up in the phone book and found my way there.

My luck turned. The owner was on the premises and eager to be of help. A tall man with a mild, cultivated air and a faint accent, he immediately produced my father's address and insisted on driving me there. As soon as we got in his car he began to apologize. He never should have gotten the police involved, and he wouldn't have if he'd known Arthur was on parole. Never! Not for a moment! He was deeply sorry for the trouble he'd caused. "Such an extraordinary man, your father. Such things he has done. The airplanes, the dam in Turkey."

"It wasn't your fault," I told him.

"Such interesting conversations we had."

He went on this way until we reached the apartment, a converted garage on the ground floor of a stucco house. I could see the ocean between two apartment buildings at the end of the street; when the store owner turned the engine off I heard the crash and surge of waves. He came around to open the trunk for me and this was when my father stepped outside. He must have seen us pull up. He looked wary, and no wonder. I had omitted to tell him I was coming, because up to the last minute I wasn't sure I'd go through with it. He hadn't seen me for six years, since I was fifteen; I did not look like that boy anymore, especially in the uniform I'd worn so I could fly military standby. At first glance I was just a stranger with badges and shiny boots, the embodiment of civic compulsion in the company of a man he had defrauded. I wouldn't have recognized him either. He wore ugly black glasses. His face had thickened, his nose gone puffy as a cauliflower. He needed a shave.

"Hello, Arthur," the store owner said. "Here is your son."

He looked at me. "Toby?"

I put my hand out. He stood there, then took it, then bent toward me and kissed me clumsily on the lips.

The store owner put my duffel bag on the sidewalk. "Let me know if you need anything," he said to me. Then, sadly, "How are you, Arthur?"

"Tops, Peter. Hunky-dory." As we watched the car pull away my father asked me how I happened to arrive with "the melancholy Dane." I began a narration, but once I came to the matter of the unpaid bill he shook his head to let me know he'd heard enough.

It was a bad beginning, and we had trouble getting past it. My father went back and forth between cuffing my arm, calling me Buster and Chum and the pet names of my childhood, and standing back with a puzzled, watchful expression. He didn't know what to do with me. Of course

I'd been a jackass to surprise him, but it went beyond that. It had to do with the whole of our history. He must have wondered where we stood in all this, what I'd forgiven, what I held against him, what I held against myself. I had questions of my own. The air between us was heavy with them.

After I'd changed clothes and had a sandwich we escaped the apartment and followed the walkway above the beach. The afternoon light glared on the water. My father noticed that I was squinting and pulled a pair of sunglasses out of his pocket. "Go on," he said, when I tried to refuse.

"What about you?"

"I'm used to it."

They were aviator glasses, the real thing, much better than the shades I'd left in the apartment. He had me put them on, take them off so he could make adjustments, put them on again. "Perfect," he said. "M-made for you. Keep 'em."

"I can't."

"They're yours. End of discussion."

I had the sense to stop arguing and after that he seemed happier to be with me. We walked and talked until he got winded and sat on a bench with his hands on his knees, looking for all the world like the old Jewish guys I used to see on the benches in Sarasota when I was a kid. Fleshy, bald, sorrow-eyed, hair bristling from their ears. That shouldn't have come as any surprise – he was an old Jewish guy, whether he admitted it or not – but I hadn't been prepared to see him in just this light. Not my father, whose physical presence could crowd a room, whose deep voice and imperial bearing had served as collateral for the most fabulous promises and claims. I never saw him do a moment's exercise, but the one time he ever really hit me – I'd asked for it – my head snapped back so hard that it shocked him even more than me, and he burst into tears. Even when I loved him, even when I despised him, there had always been a certain fear. No more. His weakening put me at ease. I waited as he collected himself, and let him set the pace on the walk home.

We had a couple of drinks when we got back. The apartment was small but he'd managed to furnish it comfortably and even with some style. I couldn't help but notice the color television, as I had earlier noticed the watch he was wearing – a Heuer chronograph that must have been worth several hundred dollars. There were other objects of value, more than could be strictly accounted for by welfare and Geoffrey's checks, but I kept my questions to myself. We washed a heap of dishes and listened to Art Tatum and got pretty loose, whereupon I suggested we go out for dinner, on me. He knew just the place. We duded ourselves up and drove there in his '53 Cadillac, which, he hurried to tell me, he'd picked up for a song.

The restaurant bar was cool and dark. We made a stop there, then proceeded to our table with fresh glasses in hand. By the time our meat arrived, thick bloody steaks served on slabs of wood, we were pretty well oiled, but that didn't stop me, with my father's judicious concurrence – "I suppose I could manage a glass" – from ordering a bottle of red.

He did indeed manage a glass. So did I. We were flush, not so much with the wine itself as with the long tangled journey we'd made to share it. My father began to preen a little. He bantered with the waiter, sent tribute to the kitchen. He exchanged greetings with our neighbors ("My boy here's in for the day, making sure the old man's keeping his nose clean . . ."). His voice grew deeper as the night went on, his phrasing and inflections more urbane. He sat up straighter, squared his great shoulders, laughed from deep in his chest as he recalled the old stories, the old names. Nothing was said about the final destination of my trip. I noticed the perfect drape of his linen jacket, the way his gold signet ring flashed in the candlelight. I could see how pleasure lightened him and restored his patrician authority. This was when I chose to ask if it was true that his family was Jewish.

He went still, the light died out of his eyes. "No," he said. "Of course not. Why?"

"I'm just curious. They were my family too, and I don't know anything about them."

"Episcopalians."

"Really? Both sides?"

"Both sides."

"What about your mother? Her maiden name was Krotoshiner, right? Isn't that a Jewish name?"

"German."

"And Wolff?"

"German. East Prussian, if you want to be particular." He looked around as if to call for the bill.

"But – correct me if I'm wrong – wasn't your mother in Hadassah?"

"Hell's bells, son, I don't know. She belonged to every g-goddamned charity in Hartford, maybe she was in that one too. Sure! Why not."

I kept after him in this falsely innocent way, as if I were just trying to clear up some minor confusions of my own, until he lost patience.

"For Christ's sake," he said, "what do you want?"

I couldn't answer him. I didn't know what I wanted. He got up and went outside while I paid the check. I thought he might very well leave me there, but he was waiting in the car, staring dead ahead. We spoke only once on the drive home, when he ran a stop sign. I pointed this out to him. Without looking at me he said, "I stopped at the last one."

The couch was a pull-out. We made up the bed in silence, then he asked if I needed anything.

"Could we have a nightcap?"

He was stiff about it but he poured a couple of drinks and put on a record.

"Hey, that's great," I said. "Who is it?"

He told me, and then told me who the sidemen were, and when it was recorded, and why it was such a hard record to find nowadays. This led him to play me several more of his treasures. He listened exactly the way Geoffrey listened, making rhythm noises, leaning forward suddenly with narrowed eyes when one of the players commenced a star solo, compelling me to listen with him. When he saw that I was fighting sleep he collected our glasses and turned off the stereo. I stood up, weaving with drink and fatigue. "Good night," I said.

"You sure you have to leave tomorrow?"

"Afraid so."

"Well, kiddo . . ." He put his arms around me and I let myself lean against him. It was a relief not to have to look into his face anymore, into his terrible sadness. We didn't say a word. I don't know how long we stood like that, but it began to seem a long time. Then I straightened up, and he let go of me.

At the replacement depot in Oakland I met up with an acquaintance from Fort Bragg, a young lieutenant with the 82nd Airborne. His name was Stu Hoffman. He was freckle-faced and skinny and excessively thoughtful. No command presence. An even more unlikely officer than I was. We weren't friends, but we used to run into each other at the officers club and talk about writing. He also had ambitions in that direction. I didn't take them very seriously because he was nuts about Thomas Wolfe, and I looked down on both Wolfe and his admirers, though I had recently admired him myself. Stu for his part didn't understand my reverence for Hemingway. Hemingway, he said, did not love words, and to be a writer you had to love words.

We were scheduled for the same flight to Vietnam. They'd given us two entire days in Oakland for outprocessing but there really wasn't that much to do, and we were free by the afternoon of the first day. We changed into civvies and caught a cab into San Francisco, to the Haight-Ashbury, to see if we could find some hippies having LSD trips. Maybe there would be a Happening or a Be-In. That was the way we proposed the excursion, gee-whizzing it up, cartooning the expectations of a pair of rubes who got their picture of the world from the Des Moines *Register*.

In fact we did find a Happening in progress, right on Haight Street, and there were hippies, and some of them gave signs of being in touch with pretty far-off places. Stu and I were issued batik headbands and embraced by each of a party of soulful wanderers who identified themselves as "the Hug Patrol." We did not laugh at them, nor at the earnest demonstrations of candlemaking and tie-dyeing, nor at the bearded, bare-chested man in harem pants who sat on a blanket with his eyes closed, playing a sitar. Their goodwill was too naked and guileless for that. They were like children playing, but more touching because they weren't children. I was embarrassed by all this determined innocence yet somehow protective of it. Made wistful. Chastened.

We tied the headbands around our cropped skulls and moseyed along the street, returning smile for smile, walking tenderly in our spit-shined low quarters as if afraid of breaking something.

Afterward we went to a bar near the Panhandle where we drank pitchers and told our stories. I talked, but Stu talked more. He'd been raised in Chicago by his father's parents, because his mother had died when he was young and his father was out of the country for weeks and even months at a time. He was a petroleum engineer. A living legend, Stu said. Mention the name Bill Hoffman to anybody in the oil game and they'd buy you a drink on the spot. The man was amazing. He'd found oil in places there wasn't supposed to be any, time and time again. And before that, before he went to college and all, he'd been a champion motorcycle racer. And a war hero, one of the original paratroopers. Jumped with General Gavin over Normandy and all the rest of it. Two Purple Hearts, a Silver Star, and a whole shitload of other medals, including some from France. De Gaulle personally pinned one on him and kissed his cheeks.

Stu had a picture of it in his room at home – Charles de Gaulle putting a lip-lock on his father.

His father was one in a million, just a little hard to talk to. He wouldn't tell you what he was thinking. You were supposed to know. When Stu decided to drop out of the Colorado School of Mines his father didn't say a word against it, though it was his own alma mater. Stu would've stuck it out to keep him happy, but he was flunking most of his courses; the only thing he ever wanted to do was read and that didn't get you very far at CSM. Anyway his father didn't say much when he quit, just, "It's your life, live it any damn way you want." When Stu enlisted in the army the most he'd say about it was, "Don't let the bastards con you into anything," and to this day he hadn't managed to congratulate him on making it through Officer Candidate School and airborne training. Stu figured he must be happy to see him keeping up the family tradition, but it just wasn't his way to show it.

Terrific guy, though. Solid as a rock.

Stu said his father was flying in the next day to see him off. He asked if I'd join them for dinner, and took it as a big favor when I said yes.

"He's great," Stu said. "Really. Just a little hard to talk to sometimes."

Later that night we tried to get into the Top of the Mark and were turned away for not wearing ties. We stood outside the Mark Hopkins and howled, "O lost, and by the wind grieved, ghost, come back again!" The doormen were our only audience, and they ignored us. They stood at parade rest in their frogged overcoats and acted as if we weren't there. They made us look like imbeciles. We moved off down the street, staggering to show how drunk we were.

I took a bus into town the next day and walked around North Beach, searching for Kerouac's old hangouts. Later I went back to the Haight. The Happening was over but I kept seeing the same credulous faces, or maybe they were different faces with the same look. Again I felt that wistfulness of the day before. Without talking to anyone except a girl who tried to sell me a belt, unconscious of my purpose in returning, I wandered the neighborhood until it was time for dinner.

We met up in a seafood restaurant down by Fishermen's Wharf. Stu had worn his uniform and looked completely implausible in the big jump boots and starched khakis covered with insignia, awkward and self-conscious, like a Boy Scout with all his merit badges on.

The first thing Mr Hoffman said to me was, "So you're the other one about to get his ass shot off."

Stu laughed miserably.

"I hope not," I said.

"Well, that'll do you no end of good," Mr Hoffman said. He didn't smile. He had freckles like Stu's and thin white lips – also freckled – and curly red hair. His skin looked taut over his high cheekbones. He ordered drinks and watched me impatiently while I answered Stu's questions about my day. I didn't mention going back to the Haight.

Mr Hoffman wanted to know what I thought of General William Childs Westmoreland.

Stu slumped in his chair. He looked tired.

"I've never met him," I said.

"You must have an opinion." Mr Hoffman broke off a piece of bread with a sharp twisting motion, the way you'd tighten a coupling. The backs of his freckled hands were covered with wiry hair. "Starting tomorrow he holds the papers on you, right? So what do you think?"

I didn't know how to answer – what he hoped to hear.

"You think he cares about you?"

I considered this. "Yes, given the exigencies of command."

"Exigencies!" He looked at Stu. "No wonder you two hit it off."

"We've been all through this, Dad."

"I'm asking your friend a simple question. You mind?" he said to me.

I looked over at Stu. He picked up the menu and started to read it.

"Stu wants to be a teacher," Mr Hoffman said. "Maybe even write some books. What do you think of that?"

"I think it's great."

"So do I. Nobody in our family has ever written a book, far as I know. He can do it too, Stu can. Stu is not your general-issue human being. But I guess you know that."

The waiter came over to take our orders. After he left, Mr Hoffman said, "Did you know that General William Childs Westmoreland ordered a parachute jump in high winds that got a whole bunch of boys killed? Broke their necks and every other damned thing. This was Fort Campbell, understand – not Vietnam. No military necessity."

"I've heard mention of it."

"And what does that tell you about General William Childs Westmoreland?"

"I don't know. It was a training jump. I guess you could say training is a military necessity."

"Would you swallow that horseshit if one of those boys was your son?"

I took a drink and set my glass down carefully.

Mr Hoffman said, "Every single one of those boys was somebody's son."

"Dad."

"He didn't lose a wink. Came out clean as a whistle. What do you owe those bastards anyway?" he said to Stu. "You think you owe them something?"

Stu closed his eyes.

"I'll tell you what he cares about, him and that sorry dickhead from Texas. *How he looks.* That's it. That is the be-all and end-all of his miserable existence."

Mr Hoffman worked this vein until our dinners came. He shoved his food around for a while and then stood and said, "Excuse us." He waited while Stu got up, and the two of them left the dining room. They were gone long enough for me to finish my dinner. Neither of them said anything when they came back. Stu didn't look at me. He sat down and began eating, stiffly, the way they made us eat in OCS, shoulders squared, eyes glazed, chewing like a machine.

Mr Hoffman took a few bites and pushed the plate away. "What does your father think?" he asked me.

"About what?"

"About you getting your ass shot off for the greater glory of Lyndon Baines Johnson and William Childs Westmoreland."

"I'm not sure. We haven't been in very close touch."

"Stu and I, we haven't been in close touch either. But

that's damn well going to change. Right, Stu?" Mr Hoffman touched his arm. Stu nodded. Mr Hoffman took his hand away and Stu went on eating.

"You ought to talk to your father," Mr Hoffman said. "He might have a thing or two to say about this."

"It doesn't look like we're going to have a chance."

"Well, that's a shame."

Mr Hoffman insisted on going upstairs to the piano bar for a drink. Three customers were sitting together at the piano, a TWA pilot and two women. When the pianist finished the song he was playing, the TWA pilot asked for "Theme from *The Apartment*." The woman to his right bumped him with her shoulder and said, "Ronnnn!" She rolled her eyes at us, miming exasperation with him for hinting at their secrets. She had a round face full of physical good nature. The pilot murmured something and she bumped him again. "You big goof," she said.

The other one looked at me just long enough to reveal how bored she was with the sight before her, then turned away. She was drooped over a cigarette, a bony blonde with a long pale neck and pouty lips.

The pianist doodled prettily around the keyboard, then entered the song. He played it with his eyes half closed. At the end he ducked his head at the applause and took a drink from a glass of milk.

The woman with the pilot leaned forward and, staring at Stu's jump wings, asked if he was in the air force. Her brother was in the air force, she said, in Guam.

"Army," Stu said. Then, with helpless pride, "Paratroops." He bent his head toward me. "Both of us."

"Been over yet?" the pilot asked.

"Tomorrow morning."

"Give 'em hell," the pilot said.

"Christ almighty," Mr Hoffman said. "I need a cigar." He slid off his stool and left the room.

The pianist started playing "It Was a Very Good Year."

I looked at Stu. "I thought he wouldn't tell you what was on his mind."

He was picking at his cocktail napkin. "It's been like this all day. Bam bam bam. Bam bam bam. He just won't let up."

"What's he so worked up about?"

"He doesn't want me to go," Stu said.

"So I gather. It's not like you have a choice."

"He doesn't see it that way."

"Come on. What're you supposed to do – desert?"

Stu didn't answer.

"What, he wants you to desert?"

Stu looked at me. He still didn't say anything.

"It's a federal offense," I said.

He grinned.

"Well, it is."

"A federal offense," Stu said. "That's great. I haven't heard that since I was a kid."

Mr Hoffman was followed back into the bar by two women in rustling evening dresses and two men wearing fancy-stitched Western suits with bolo ties, pointy boots, and bronc-buster belt buckles. Their entry had the quality of a stampede. They came in and milled around, the women rubbing their arms in the chill of the air-conditioning, the men bellowing at each other and rocking back on their heels to fire bursts of laughter toward the ceiling. They

found their way to the piano and set up a trading post —
purses, piles of coins, wallets, cigarettes, lighters in silver-
and-turquoise cases. The women wore a lot of brilliant
jewelry. All four of them ordered margaritas and smiled
around at the rest of us to show we had nothing to fear.

When the pianist played "The Yellow Rose of Texas,"
one of the women whooped. "Listen to him! You're in the
wrong state, mister." She finally let on they were from
Arizona.

Stu leaned over to me. "We're gonna split. You coming?"

I looked across the piano at the snooty blonde. She was
staring into her drink.

"You go on," I said. "Catch you in the morning."

Mr Hoffman gave my shoulder a squeeze, and they
were gone.

The Arizonans had the pianist play "Hello, Dolly," and
made the rest of us join in. One of the men draped his arm
around the blonde and swayed back and forth with her. She
didn't pull away but she didn't sing, either. She smiled in a
tight-lipped way like someone with bad teeth.

We sang a few show tunes, then the Wild Bunch rolled
up their sleeves: "Don't Fence Me In," "Cool Water,"
"Tumbling Tumbleweeds." It was their party now. They
kept our glasses full and made sure we were loud enough.
The blonde left. She didn't say good-bye to anyone, just got
up and left. I wanted to sneak out after her but I couldn't
find the right moment. We drank to the approaching
nuptials of the pilot and his girlfriend. We drank to the
piano player. We drank to the Cactus State, and to the
States United. We sang some patriotic songs and everybody
got choked up.

Then the pilot told the Arizonans I was shipping out
the next morning. One of the women took this as an
occasion to shed tears. Her husband patted her on the
back a few times, then he and his friend took seats
beside me and settled down to the business of giving
me advice.

Jovial men get serious with a vengeance. It lurks there
always behind their crinkled eyes, the eagerness to show
you that even if they do know how to have a good time
they can by God get down to cases too. These weren't the
worst of the breed. They professed no gospel, no dietary
plan, no road to riches. But all the same I could see how
happy they were to close the party down, to pull long faces
and speak of arms and war.

Both were vets and had plenty to say, though I couldn't
follow much of it. "This country can mobilize!" one of them
kept shouting. Finally the wives took pity on me and made
them stop. Then we were all out on the street in glistening
fog, shaking hands and embracing, promising to meet again,
next year in Phoenix. The men guided me into a cab. As
the driver counted the money they'd given him, one of
them leaned inside and regarded me solemnly. "Son," he
said. I could see he wanted to say something, something
momentous. I bent toward him. He said, "Keep your head
down, son."

I lay awake in my room until the orderly called me. It was
still dark when we boarded the buses. A sergeant got on
and read our names out. Stu didn't answer. Neither did
two other men. When the sergeant came to the end of his
list he called their names again, then asked if anyone knew

why they weren't present. Silence. He made a notation on his clipboard and got off the bus.

They kept the inside lights off on the way to the airport. Cigarettes burned in the gloom. Hardly anyone spoke, and then just a few words, quietly. There was no grab-ass, no swagger. Later, on the plane, we'd find our tongues and talk ourselves into a grotesquely festive state, but at this moment we were numbed by the grip of the current that was carrying us away. I was, anyway. Until now nothing had seemed irrevocable. I had persisted in the unconscious faith that no matter what I did, no matter how many steps I took, I would be excused from taking this last step. Something would happen – I didn't know what. The VC would surrender. My orders would get changed. The President would decide to pull out. Something. Up to now men had been going over in one long unbroken line, but I hadn't been one of them. My position in the line guaranteed that something would happen to make it stop. I hadn't really thought these things but I must have felt them, because I was in shock to find myself on the bus that morning, and I don't believe it was just my imagination that the others were in shock too.

We weren't meant to be here, every one of us knew that, but here we were.

An odd question came to me, one I've never forgotten. What would this bus look like if you could see us all exactly as we would be a year from now?

Nothing could stop it. Except . . . what? A breakdown? We'd just have to get on another bus. My pals from the Haight – the Hug Patrol in a human chain across the road? Nah, bunch of softies, they'd never get up this early.

Hijackers. A gang of hijackers in front of a barricade, wielding shotguns and pitchforks and clubs, shining bright lights into the driver's eyes. The driver stops. The hijackers pound on the door until he opens it. They come up the steps and down the aisle, flashing their beams from face to face until they find the ones they're after. They call our names, and then we know who it is behind the blinding lights. It's our fathers. Our fathers, come to take us home.

Crazy.

But not as crazy as what they actually did, which was let us go.

PART TWO

The Lesson

They had been coming into My Tho for weeks. The Vietnamese army didn't know, the American advisers didn't know. The town was full of them and nobody said a word. I couldn't forget that afterward – not a word of warning from anyone. For weeks they were all around us, on the streets, in the restaurants, gathering for the great slaughter and tasting the pleasures of the town until it began.

Certain scenes acquire piquancy in afterthought. Just before Tet a carnival established itself in a park along the river. Sergeant Benet and I stopped there one night and wandered among the games, the puppet shows, the jugglers and fire eaters. There was a dinky shooting gallery with a couple of antique .22s, and I lingered to try my hand. A stoop-shouldered man, tall for a Vietnamese, took the place to my right. A pair of younger fellows stood behind him and cheered him on. He shot well. So did I. We didn't acknowledge that we were competing, but we were, definitely. Then I missed some and quit for fear I'd miss more. "Good shooting," I said to him. He inclined his head and smiled. It might have been an innocent smile, but I think of it now as a complicated, terrible smile.

By pure dumb luck I was in my bunk at the battalion

when the killing started. If I'd been in town or on the road, *end of story*. The first American they killed was a young guy from headquarters who was driving home from a bar after midnight. He probably felt safe because of the annual holiday cease-fire. They caught him on the road and shot him. Instead of leaving his body, they lugged it around for the entire time they held My Tho. Maybe they thought he'd prove valuable in some future exchange of the dead, or maybe they just couldn't bring themselves to part with such a trophy. He was very big. In the end they did get some use out of him, as a kind of portable bulwark to hide behind and shoot from. When his body was found afterward, Doc Macleod told me, "he was so full of holes you could have played him like a fucking ocarina."

They were happy to kill any Americans who fell into their hands but they were more efficient at killing Vietnamese. They'd come prepared with lists of local politicians, teachers, civil servants, anyone named by their agents as insufficiently friendly to the cause. Early that morning, when they could count on the people's enemies being asleep in their beds, execution squads went from door to door, rounding them up. Meanwhile their political cadres took control of the streets and their sappers began to attack police stations and military barracks. All this we found out later. When the assault, the so-called Tet Offensive, first began we didn't know what was going on.

The firing woke us up. It was about three-thirty, four in the morning, January 31, 1968, which I think of now as a kind of birthday; the first day in the rest of my life, for sure. Sergeant Benet and I hustled outside and saw flares going up all over the town. Soldiers from the battalion were running past us, carbines in hand, heading for the perimeter. I said I didn't like this. I could hear myself say it: "I don't like this."

We got dressed and walked over to Major Chau's headquarters. His staff officers were carrying out tables and chairs, map cases, radios. One of them told the major we were there. He came to the door and said, "Later. You come back later." When I asked him for a situation report, he said, "Later. Now is too busy, yes," and went back inside.

Sergeant Benet and I spent the morning cleaning our weapons and listening to the radio. In this way we learned that My Tho was in enemy hands and most of our division under attack. We also found out that the same thing was happening everywhere else. All the towns of the Delta — My Tho, Ben Tre, Soc Trang, Can Tho, Ca Mau, Vinh Long, all of them — were full of VC. Every town and city in the country was under siege. Every airfield had been hit. Every road cut. They were in the streets of Saigon, in the American embassy. All in one night. The whole country.

I could barely take in what I was hearing. To make sense of it was especially hard because nothing could be put to use, or translated into hope. Even the official optimism of the Armed Forces Radio announcers couldn't patch over the magnitude of the facts they were reporting, and when we tuned in the regular military frequencies we heard nothing but shock and frenzied pleas for support. Nobody was getting any support because the supporting units needed support themselves. That meant we couldn't get relief from anyone, which was sorry news for us. The battalion was undermanned to begin with, and a lot of our troops had gone home for Tet. We would have to defend this ridiculously exposed piece of land with a skeleton crew and without a prayer of hell from the air or the ground. We were completely on our own.

Sergeant Benet and I listened to the radio and said little. He was lying on the couch, gazing up at the ceiling, which was a kindness. I didn't want him to see how I was taking this because I didn't really know how I was taking it. I felt as if I were looking on from a great distance. As the morning passed I got hungry and made a sandwich, still listening. I became aware of my hands and what they were doing. How strange it is to spread mayonnaise. It can be the strangest thing you've ever done. I ate a few bites and had to stop, my mouth was so dry.

Major Chau sent for us. He was in the bunker where he'd set up his command post. "This is too bad," he said. "You can get air support, yes?"

"No. Nothing."

"Yes! Come. Look." He showed me the map, tapping with his pointer, trying to make me see the difficulty of our position. When he finally understood that I couldn't call down jets if we were attacked, he made a hissing noise and bared his teeth. He laid the pointer on the map and fumbled out a Marlboro but couldn't fit it into the holder he used. He looked down at the cigarette and the holder, then turned and walked outside. A few minutes later he came back and acted as if nothing had happened. Sergeant Benet and I leaned over the map with him and his staff officers, trying to imagine a plan of some kind, but none of us had anything much to say.

I felt hollow, loopy. I was dull and slow-tongued, the

others as well. What we did was stand around and wait for something to happen.

All this time we could hear the sound of the shooting in My Tho.

A shell exploded somewhere outside. We hit the deck, our mouths twisted in dire grins. Two more went off almost together. They weren't very close, but I felt the shock in my chest. We waited for the next one. Then we stood up again, very, very slowly. I was wide awake.

Later that afternoon a soldier came to the door of the bunker and said there was an airplane above us. It turned out to be a spotter plane, a small single-engine craft like a Piper Cub. The pilot was circling the battalion and wagging his wings as if he wanted something. Sergeant Benet flipped through the radio until he found his frequency.

The pilot was in a state of some impatience. He'd been flying past, he said, and seen a large body of men moving up behind one of the tree lines that faced our perimeter, about three football fields away. He wasn't sure how many, could be a hundred, hundred fifty of them. We couldn't see anybody but he gave us their position and kept circling above to direct fire.

Everyone went to work. Major Chau was a good artilleryman. He'd long ago had his fire-direction people work out the range on that spot and on every other likely avenue of attack, and they fed the settings to the men waiting in the gun pits. The gun crews fired three salvos in rapid succession. I watched the shells bursting in the trees and thought, Yes! Yes! We caught them all bunched up together. The pilot had a high, thin voice that cracked with excitement as he told us how we were killing them – "knocking them down," as he put it. We adjusted and fired for effect, round after round after round, mud geysering up, trees toppling and exploding into flame. When the VC broke and ran the pilot followed them, calling down more fire, yipping like a cowboy every time we knocked more of them down. The tree line was long and dense. We could hear our shells exploding in the paddies behind it but never saw any of the men we were killing until the end, when a few of them hooked left and made a run for the My Tho road. They crossed our line of vision for a few moments then, five or six distant figures in black loping in a half crouch across the tops of the dikes. The sight of them astonished me. I went absolutely blank. The perimeter guards let off a clatter of shots but didn't hit anyone. They made the road and vanished over the embankment.

The pilot let them go. He had us concentrate our fire on the larger group we couldn't see until they were down or dispersed into cover. Then he gave us the all clear and climbed away. When Sergeant Benet thanked him he didn't answer, just wagged his wings.

We let the guns cool. Then – flushed, giddy, ears ringing, teeth clenched in weird elation – we commenced firing again. We were thin on the ground but we had a mountain of ammunition. All that afternoon we fired, and on into the night. I say *we*. In truth I did very little. My advice was not in demand. An American who couldn't get choppers or jets had no vote. When I got tired of hanging around the command bunker I checked the perimeter posts and helped Sergeant Benet hump ammo and clear the pits of shell casings. Sergeant Benet worked himself into a lather. Stripped to the waist, skin gleaming, shouting encouragement to the gunners, he loomed like Vulcan in the sulfurous smoke and din. As darkness came on, the tips of the barrels glowed like embers.

We blew up the road leading from My Tho so they couldn't attack us with the trucks and armored personnel carriers they'd seized. We blew up the surrounding tree lines to deny them cover and the dikes so they couldn't use them as trails. We blew up the landings along the river. Wherever they might move or hide in the countryside around us we dropped high explosives. Then we turned our attention to the town.

The process by which we helped lay waste to My Tho seemed not of our making and at all times necessary and right. As the battalions in town came under more and more pressure, we began to drop shells on the buildings around them. We bombarded the old square surrounding General Ngoc's headquarters, where he and the province chief were holed up with their staff officers. There were pockets of terrified government officialdom and soldiery huddled throughout the town, and every time one of them got through to us on the radio we put our fire right where he wanted it, no questions asked. We knocked down bridges and sank boats. We leveled shops and bars along the river. We pulverized hotels and houses, floor by floor, street by street, block by block. I saw the map, I knew where the shells were going, but I didn't think of our targets as homes where exhausted and frightened people were praying for their lives. When you're afraid you will kill anything that might kill you. Now that the enemy had the town, the town was the enemy.

And I wasn't too sure about our friends. I worried that Major Chau and his officers might run out on us if we got attacked, maybe even cut a deal and hand us over. These men had never given me any reason for such a thought, as I well knew, but that didn't stop me from thinking it.

For the next couple of days we plastered the town. Then the jets showed up. Their run into My Tho took them right over our compound, sometimes low enough that we could see the rivets on their skin. Such American machines, so boss-looking, so technical, so loud. *Phantoms*. When they slowed overhead to lock into formation the roar of their engines made speech impossible. Down here I was in a deranged and malignant land, but when I raised my eyes to those planes I could see home. They dove screaming on the town, then pulled out and banked around and did it again. Their bombs sent tremors pulsing up through our legs. When they used up all their bombs they flew off to get more. Flames gleamed on the underside of the pall of smoke that overhung My Tho, and the smell of putrefaction soured the breeze, and still we served the guns, dropping rings of ruination around every frightened man with a radio transmitter.

None of this gave me pause. Only when we finally took the town back, when the last sniper had been blasted off his rooftop, did I see what we had done, we and the VC together. The place was a wreck, still smoldering two weeks later, still reeking sweetly of corpses. The corpses were everywhere, lying in the streets, floating in the reservoir, buried and half buried in collapsed buildings, grinning, blackened, fat with gas, limbs missing or oddly bent, some headless, some burned almost to the bone, the smell so thick and foul we had to wear surgical masks scented with cologne, aftershave, deodorant, whatever we had, simply to move through town. Hundreds of corpses and the count kept rising. Gangs of diggers sifted through the rubble, looking for survivors. They found some, but mostly they found more corpses. These they rolled up in tatami mats and left by the roadside for pickup. One day I passed a line of them that went on for almost a block, all children, their bare feet protruding from the ends of the mats. My driver told me that we'd bombed a school building where they had been herded together to learn revolutionary history and songs.

I didn't believe it. It sounded like one of those stories that always make the rounds afterward. But it could have been true.

Now that the danger was past I could permit myself certain feelings about what we had done, but I knew even then that they would vanish at the next sign of danger. How about the VC? I used to wonder. Were they sorry? Did they love their perfect future so much that they could without shame feed children to it, children and families and towns – their own towns? They must have, because they kept doing it. And in the end they got their future. The more of their country they fed to it, the closer it came.

As a military project Tet failed; as a lesson it succeeded. The VC came into My Tho and all the other towns knowing what would happen. They knew that once they were among the people we would abandon our pretense of distinguishing between them. We would kill them all to get at one. In this way they taught the people that we did not love them and would not protect them; that for all our talk of partnership and brotherhood we disliked and mistrusted them, and that we would kill every last one of them to save our own skins. To believe otherwise was self-deception. They taught that lesson to the people, and also to us. At least they taught it to me.

Old China

I met Pete Landon when I was in language school. Pete was a Foreign Service officer, educated at Groton and Harvard, very talented, very accomplished. He already spoke French, German, and Italian, and while everyone else was still rendering Vietnamese as if it were some absurd mutation of English he'd begun learning its poetry. He was athletic and rakish. Other men, myself among them, courted his notice as if he were a beautiful girl; he had that charge of glamour. When he laughed at something I said, I felt lucky. Singled out.

Pete was seven or eight years my senior and showed an avuncular interest in me that I was not above encouraging with stories of near-death experiences during survival training and parachute jumps. He seemed amused by my impersonation of a cocky young warrior, and I played it up.

Pete got to Vietnam before I did and spent some months in the countryside. Then he was posted to Saigon. He sent me his address and offered a bed whenever I needed one, an invitation I put to use several times when I came to town on supply missions. His house was a handsome old villa surrounded by gardens and

137

serviced by a gardener, several cleaning women, and a French-trained cook.

Pete had four roommates, also civilians. I didn't know what any of them actually did and I had the idea I shouldn't press them on the subject. They were smart, casually elegant guys from the same world as Pete, and, like him, princely in their hospitality. They always had friends in the house, journalists, visitors from the States, cryptic young officers from up-country wearing Montagnard bracelets. It was like an ultracool fraternity.

We assembled before dinner and put on some music and cracked open the scotch. The music got louder, we got louder. Pete and his friends were close about their work but dedicated gossips with a familial range of common acquaintance. They spoke, it seemed to me, not as snobs but as canny observers of their tribe. What else would they talk about? As they drank and matched stories, the world they conjured up became more real and present than the world outside the house, and they became part of it again. I could see it happen. It happened to me too, through an old trick of longing by which I managed to believe myself one of them.

Dinner was formal. This formality did not extend to dress, but it governed the protocols of speech and conduct. We were young men, after all, flushed with drink, trembling on the edge of riot. It was understood that the night would end orgiastically. The polite forms postponed that conclusion while respecting its inevitability, making every decorum an aspect of the debauchery yet to come.

We sat at a mahogany table lit by two silver candelabra. Pete presided, carving the meat, explaining the wine, conducting us like a choirmaster. He ruled but did not oppress. He managed to get each of us to put something on exhibit, to recite Shakespeare or sing a song or tell a story he knew we told well. When we finished he'd say "Hear, hear!" As the meal went on he pinged his glass and stood to propose toasts so long-winded and mannered that I assumed he must be parodying someone, maybe even parodying toasts themselves, the very idea of toasts, toasts as the ur-liturgy of that exquisite respectability whose restraints we would soon be trashing. Once we'd eaten our fill he did not suffer us to hurry away. He produced cognac and Cuban cigars and leaned back in his chair, thinking deep, inviting us to consider whether the Novel really was dead, and if Napoleon's Russian campaign had in fact been such a great failure as conventional minds made it out to be. In the best Socratic fashion – "Good point, well taken, but is there perhaps another way of thinking about Borodino?" – he held us to the subject until there was nothing left of it or of our capacity to spout this guff, and then he'd fold his napkin and push back his chair and suggest that perhaps we might get a drink somewhere.

How bizarre, to enter the streets of Saigon after a night at Pete's table. Everything was newly foreign: the buildings, the look of the trees against the evening sky, the sounds and smells, and most of all the people in their absolute otherness, crowds of them on the sidewalks and roads, under awnings, in doorways and restaurants, so many it seemed they must be out for some purpose. We worked our way among them to the street, flagged cabs, and began our descent into the night.

Given the daunting standards of the time and place, there

was nothing remarkable in our dissipation; only, perhaps, in the feeling of superiority that joined us while we pursued it. Back in the house we'd kept the forms of gentility with the understanding that they didn't really own us. We were renegades; this young gentlemen business was irony. But later, in the dumps where our outlaw trail led us, the irony assumed another form. We were, it seemed, young gentlemen after all, drawn here by anthropological curiosity. This heightened sense of ourselves gave us both license and detachment. We were on the Grand Tour, and this was part of its truth, which we as touristical swells had a duty to eat whole without making faces.

Pete controlled the itinerary. He drank but didn't show it. His speech never thickened or slurred, his manner became more old-world as the night ran its course. When the rest of us were at the point of collapse Pete caused taxis to appear and carry us back to the villa. At this moment he was at his brightest and most affable. He was ready to scramble up some eggs, brew a pot of coffee, have a serious talk.

The others waved him off and went to bed. But I stayed up with Pete. I liked having his attention; it was worth losing some sleep for. He ransacked the kitchen for sweet rolls and cakes and urged them on me with an open hand, along with his thoughts and advice. I knew he had two kid brothers back home; he treated me pretty much as if I were one of them. And if he condescended, if he gave his advice a little too freely, if he sometimes made me feel too smartly the differences in our ages, our histories and prospects, that was all right. I knew he had my best interests at heart.

Not long after Tet, Pete paid me a visit at my battalion. He had with him in his Land-Rover a man named Shaw. They'd driven down from Saigon, hoping to reach Ben Tre, but the roads were all jammed up and when they found themselves outside My Tho in a hard rain they decided to stop for the night.

Shaw went inside to take a shower but Pete still wasn't ready to call it a day. He had Sergeant Benet and me put on our ponchos and show him around the battalion. We inspected the gun emplacements, then walked the perimeter, with Pete stopping at every strongpoint to question the guards. They deferred instantly to him, grinning like children at the miracle of his beautiful Vietnamese while he asked them about their weapons and defensive procedures and then about their home villages and families. Sergeant Benet and I waited dumbly, shoulders hunched against the drenching rain, ropy streams of it running off our hoods and past our faces.

It was dark when we got back inside. Shaw had the news on TV. Pete played with Canh Cho awhile, then came over to the kitchen area, where Sergeant Benet was making a salad while I grilled some steaks.

"*Quel boeuf!*" he said. "Filet mignon . . . Where in the world did you find those?"

"Friends," I said.

"You're doing all right here," Pete said. "The veritable lap of luxury." He didn't make this sound like a compliment.

During dinner it came out that Shaw was also a Foreign Service officer, stationed in Thailand. I liked him. He came quickly to the point and had a brusque, undeceived way of bringing you to yours. He'd traveled to Vietnam for a visit and Pete was taking time off to show him around, put him in the picture. It was a friendly thing to do, but I could see they weren't really friends. There was constraint in Shaw's manner toward Pete. He didn't seem to notice how winning Pete was and refused to be conducted in his presentation of himself, to have his gruff persona managed.

Pete didn't know how to talk to him. But he wouldn't give up; he kept bantering on in that gallant mock-courtly way of his. I had never seen Pete at a loss before. I was embarrassed for him and felt somehow disloyal in my embarrassment.

We stayed up and had a beer after Shaw and Sergeant Benet hit the rack.

"So," Pete said. "You've got yourself quite the little nest here."

"We do what we can."

"I had a somewhat different idea of your situation."

"We never really talked about it. There's not much to say."

"I mean, good Lord, you're really set up. *Entre nous*, where'd you get that TV?"

"A trade," I said.

"Really. Well. You've set yourself up in style here. Nothing left to chance."

"You're doing okay yourself," I said.

"In Saigon, yes. I didn't live that way in the bush."

I knew this was true. I had seen the photographs of Pete with his villagers, Pete sinking a well, Pete building a bridge, Pete out on patrol with the local reaction force. Pete in native garb, eating cross-legged on a dirt floor, chopsticks poised above his rice bowl. He had a thick album of these pictures, and still more framed on the walls of his bedroom.

"I would have thought you'd be traveling with a faster crowd," he said. "Something a little more out on the edge."

"You go where they send you."

"I mean, this is just like home, isn't it?"

"Not exactly."

"Oh, but it is. *Exactly.* You get tired of the old filet mignon, you pop into town for a little Chinese."

I said, "You don't just pop into My Tho."

"Well, of course you do! I thought you'd want to be out . . ." – he waved vaguely – "doing some damage."

"I've been out." Then I said, "I can't say I did much damage."

Pete leaned forward. His expression was kindly. "You know, this isn't going to last forever. You have to ask yourself: What am I going to have to remember when it's over? What am I going to have to look back on?"

I didn't know what to say.

He reached over and slapped my knee. "You're a razor-edged weapon, remember? Terror from the sky. Death on cat's feet. Don't you want to show your stuff?"

"I want to get home." The words came so fast I almost choked on them.

Pete sat back. He made as if to speak, then shook his head and took a drink. When I said good night he raised the bottle without looking at me.

The next morning Pete announced a change of plan. Instead of going on to Ben Tre, which wasn't much to look at since Tet, he proposed to drive to a village west of us to meet someone really interesting. This man had

143

held important posts throughout the Delta, and though he was now living in retirement he kept in touch with his old network and knew things about the country no one else knew. He was famous for his grasp of the situation. If he didn't know about it, it wasn't worth knowing.

Sergeant Benet said, "It's not a good road out that way."

"Nonsense," Pete said. "It's a perfectly good road. I've driven it many times."

"The surface is all right," I said. "It's just not very secure right now. Nobody uses it much."

"If nobody's using it," Pete said, "then they won't be expecting anybody, will they?"

"Probably not," I said.

Shaw was looking from one to the other of us. "How far is this place?"

"Around twenty-five clicks," I said.

"Twenty at the most." Pete looked at me. "Please don't feel obliged to go. I'm sure you have pressing things to do here."

Until that moment I'd had no thought of making the trip; it hadn't even crossed my mind. "I was hoping to go," I said.

"You don't have to."

"I want to."

"Don't do this on my account," Shaw said. "There's no need."

I shook my head. "Curiosity."

"Good man," Pete said.

Pete had to make some calls to Saigon. While he was over at

the communications center I piled sandbags on the floor of the Land-Rover and fixed us up with weapons. Two M-16s, plenty of ammo, a bunch of frags. Pete had brought his Swedish K, a good-looking, much-sought-after rifle, but only one clip. I asked Shaw if he knew how to use any of this hardware. He said he did, but preferred not to. "I'm planning to stay noncombatant on this trip," he said.

"You might have to change your plan."

"I hope not," he said.

"Are you a Quaker?"

"What a peculiar question. Why do you ask?"

"Something about the way you said 'noncombatant.' "

"What a place. You say the word noncombatant, you get asked if you're a Quaker."

"You're not, then."

"Nope."

"No offense meant."

"None taken. I can think of worse things to be."

"Not me," I said. "Not over here."

Sergeant Benet pulled me aside before we left. He didn't think I should be going. I had no orders and no mission to perform.

I said I wanted to go.

"Begging your pardon, sir, you got no business down there." He waited for my answer, and when I repeated that I wanted to go, he said "Bullshit" and turned away. It was the only time he ever swore at me.

After we'd driven a few kilometers beyond My Tho the countryside changed. The paddies were empty. Nobody tried to sell us anything, the kids didn't beg and chase after us. There were no military vehicles on the road, only a few mopeds and bicycles. The bridges were unguarded. I sat in back and kept track of our position on the map while Pete drove and pointed things out to Shaw.

Along the way we stopped to look at a brick building that had been all shot up. An acrid smell still clung to the walls. We wandered around inside, looking up at the sky through the holes in the roof. Shaw stood beside a window and began to snap pictures. Still taking pictures, he went into a crouch. I came up behind him and saw what the camera was getting, the pile of spent shells under the window, the blasted window frame, the country outside clear to the horizon, too much of it to hold at bay, though some poor soul had desperately tried. This picture was the story of his desperation.

We reached the village just before noon. Pete sent a boy with a carton of Marlboros to announce our arrival, and not long afterward we were sitting on the floor of a large, dim room with Ong Loan, the man Pete had spoken of. Ong Loan was small even for a Vietnamese, bald, and very old. He didn't look that old – his face was smooth and round, babyish – but you could hear it in his voice. He spoke in a papery whisper. Conversation must have been painful for him, but he didn't spare himself. He asked after our health, commented on the season, answered Pete's questions as to his own well-being. He spoke in his own tongue and occasionally in French; if he knew English he gave no sign of it. As he talked he held a cigarette pinched between thumb and forefinger, drew deeply on it, and with his eyes closed blew smoke toward the ceiling.

A number of people had gathered in the room with us. They stood along the walls, watching, saying nothing. After

a time two women came forward with tea and rice cakes.
Ong Loan apologized for the plainness of the fare. Pete
praised its quality.

Ong Loan asked Pete about Saigon. It had been so long,
he said, since his last visit. Years. Pete described how busy
it was, how crowded; how overrun with soldiers. I kept
expecting them to exhaust the civilities and get down
to business, to discuss those important matters of which
Ong Loan had such intimate knowledge. But no. They
went on in this pleasant humor, Ong Loan whispering
the questions, Pete answering in his liquid, idiomatic
Vietnamese. I lost them for long stretches, then picked
them up again at a familiar word or phrase. Shaw swiveled
his head from side to side as he listened. Of course he didn't
understand a word.

And then they began to discuss porcelain – Chinese
porcelain. I knew that Pete had some expertise here. The
house in Saigon was filled with books on the subject, and he
owned a collection of valuable plates and jars he'd picked
up cheap from dealers who were out of their depth. Pete
described one of his recent acquisitions to Ong Loan, who
bent forward and turned his head slightly. He forgot to
smoke. It seemed that he too was an enthusiast.

I couldn't follow them. There was no point in trying.
Like Shaw, I could only watch, and mostly I watched Pete.
More than ever I was struck by his fluency, not just in the
flow of his words but in the motion of his hands and the set
of his mouth; the way he ate and took his tea; his elaborate
courtesies. He did it all with such a flourish, such evident
pleasure – how happy and assured he was in his possession
of these people's admiration, how stylishly at home in this

147

alien place, on this hard floor, surrounded by wonder-struck villagers. Yet I could see that his greatest pleasure came not from mastery of this situation but from our observation of his mastery.

I watched him, and understood why he'd brought us here. He wanted us to see how easily he could take his place among these people, to be one of them and at the same time not one of them, yet not quite one of us. Something more than either. And his demonstration of mastery required that we be stripped of it, made helpless, reduced to the role of spectators.

Not that Pete saw it that way. He probably thought he was exposing Shaw to valuable atmospherics. But whether he knew it or not, that's what this whole number was about: the perfect Vietnamese, the compulsion to excite native awe, the insouciant gamble of life, the porcelain collection, the Swedish fucking K rifle. It was about cutting a figure.

We drank more tea. My butt was numb, my back hurt, my legs burned with cramp from being crossed so long. I didn't say anything, though. Shaw had begun to show signs of impatience and I figured he would break first. He kept shifting creakily. When this didn't get Pete's attention he simply stood up.

Pete raised his hand in acknowledgment but went on talking.

"I'm ready," Shaw said.

"We're almost done," Pete said.

"I'm ready now," Shaw said.

Pete made sumptuous apologies for the haste in which he was forced to depart, apologies Ong Loan declined even to hear. He spoke to one of the women behind us, who left

148

the room and returned with a blue-and-white bowl on a
wooden base. It was about the size of a rice bowl. Ong
Loan presented it to Pete. Pete tried to give it back, and
when this was not allowed he closed his eyes and made
a deep bow over the bowl and began to speak of Ong
Loan's incomparable largesse. It looked like we were in for
a profound experience of mandarin gratitude. I gathered up
our weapons and ammunition. Shaw followed me outside
into the rain.

"What was all that about?" Shaw said.

"You'll have to ask Pete," I told him. "It was too fast
for me."

We sat in the Land-Rover and listened to the rain tap
against the canvas top. The wind picked up. The rain fell
harder. The sky darkened, and a great blinding sheet of
water broke against the windshield. Early afternoon, and
the sky was black as night.

Through the blur of rain I saw Pete appear in the
doorway. In one hand he held a package. He scanned
the sky, then ran for the Land-Rover. Shaw pushed the
door open for him and Pete fell inside, laughing, drenched
to the skin. He handed the package back to me. "Guard
this with your life," he said. "It's worth more."

"We've got ourselves one hell of a storm here," Shaw
said.

"Not so bad," Pete said. "It'll break."

He drove fast, bent over the wheel, into the blackness.
Our headlights glared back at us from the glassy wall of
falling rain. The rain drummed on the rooftop. The air
inside the Rover grew rank and steamy; Pete had to keep
wiping the glass with his sleeve. I couldn't see well enough

to track us on the map, but it didn't matter because the radio was useless. Nothing but static.

Pete looked at me in the rearview. "Why so glum?"

"Who's glum? So what did Ong Loan have to say?"

"Ong Loan," he said, pensively. "An original. A true original."

"So what's the news? Are we winning?"

"I've got some news for you," he said. "Are you ready for it?" When I didn't answer he reached back and shook my boot. "Come on, boy! Let's see some enthusiasm! Uncle Pete's been working for you!"

I waited.

"I talked to General Reed this morning. He's going to take care of your problem."

"What problem is that?"

"Missing out on all the fun. Pack your bags, big guy — you're going to the party."

I said, "I'm not sure I understand you."

"Sure you do."

He was right; I did. I waited a moment, then said, "What, am I getting transferred?"

"Kid's got a mind like a steel trap," Pete said to Shaw.

Shaw turned in his seat and looked at him as if he'd never seen him before.

"You should have your orders by the end of the week," Pete said.

"Where to?"

"Up north. Very interesting slot, just came open. A-team."

I leaned forward between the seats. "You already set this up? This is definite?"

"A done deal. We're checking you out of the Plaza."

"I wish you'd said something to me about it."

Pete didn't answer.

I sat back again.

For ten months now I'd been telling myself that whatever luck I enjoyed was no fault of mine. I'd volunteered for the whole nine yards, and they'd chosen to put me here. This fact had allowed me to half absolve myself of the suspicion, held so far only by myself, of malingering. But now the bet was called. This was a chance to offer myself up and put all doubt to rest, and I found I had no heart for it. The knowledge was humiliating. It left me with no protection against myself.

We went through a hamlet. An old man was hunched in a doorway, smoking a cigarette. American voices broke through the fuzz on the radio, then faded again.

"Pete? I'd like to talk to you about this."

"What's wrong?" Pete said. "Afraid to leave the big guns?"

Shaw was looking straight ahead. I had the feeling he was trying to efface himself, to grant me privacy, as if I were naked.

I said, "If we could have a word together."

"Sure. All the words you want. But this is going to happen."

The rain stopped just after we reached the battalion. I invited them to spend another night, but Pete wanted to press on to Saigon.

"Pete," I said. "A word?"

Shaw headed toward the hooch. "I'll be inside," he said.

151

Pete watched him go. He had an air of puzzlement and injury, of being insufficiently appreciated. It was clear that he'd expected both of us to admire this trick of being able to yo-yo a man from one end of Vietnam to the other with a single telephone call.

"I wish you'd talked to me before you went ahead with this," I said.

"We talked last night."

"I never said I wanted a transfer."

"But of course you want a transfer! You're wasted down here."

"This is where they sent me. I took my chances like everyone else. They could've sent me anywhere. They could've sent me to this interesting slot of yours."

"They should have."

"But they didn't. That's the breaks, just the same as if they'd sent me up north. It's just the way things fell out."

"It was a mistake. Now we're fixing it. You'll thank me someday. This is the chance of a lifetime."

"I don't see it that way."

"You don't have to like it," he said. "That's not the point."

"I'm lucky I made it this far."

"It's all set," he said.

"Fine. It's all set. I understand that. I'm just not sure what I'm supposed to accomplish up there in two months. It took me longer than that to get things scooped out down here."

"Two months? Who said anything about two months?"

"That's when my tour's up."

"Come on."

152

"Less than two months."

He stared at me.

"Fifty-four and a wake-up," I said.

"You've been here ten months already?"

"Ten and change."

"Then why didn't you say something?"

"You didn't ask."

"Well, for Christ's sake! You can't go up there for two months, they'll still be breaking you in and then you're heading back home. I'll never hear the end of it. I don't suppose you'd consider extending."

I shook my head.

"You know, I used up a very big favor with General Reed getting this spot for you. What's going to happen the next time I have to ask him for something?"

I had no answer.

"If you had even four months left I'd ram this thing through anyway," Pete said. "For your own good."

I was undressing to take a shower when I found his package in the pocket of my fatigue jacket. I stashed it, figuring I'd have Sergeant Benet drop it off at Pete's villa the next time we went up to Saigon. But in the morning a message came over the battalion teletype, instructing me to put extra padding on the package and take it to the My Tho airstrip and send it out in the priority mailbag. The message concluded: DO NOT DELAY REPEAT DO NOT DELAY. This was followed by Pete's name and the acronym and postal code of his place of work.

I took the parcel out of my footlocker and weighed it in my hand. When I pinched the puffy wrapping I could feel the outline of the bowl. I didn't remember exactly what it looked like, its particular marks and patterns, but I still retained an impression of its beauty. Surely it struck everyone with its beauty when it was first brought into the room. No one had spoken; we simply watched as the bowl was handed from the old woman to Ong Loan and then to Pete. That it was ancient I knew at a glance. The blue was soft and watery, the white subtly yellowed like old ivory. To see it cupped in the hand, and then to see it given into another hand, was to understand that it was meant for that purpose; to be passed on. Pete's bow had been cinematic but I couldn't blame him for it. That he should bow in his pleasure at so antique and beautiful a thing was only right.

I put the package on the floor and pressed at it with my stockinged foot, for better control and so as not to leave any bootprints. It was tougher than I'd expected, but then of course it was tough. How else could it have lasted all those years? I gave it more and more of my weight until I was almost standing on it. Though I didn't hear the break, I felt it travel up my leg – a sudden, sad release. I picked up the package and checked to make sure I hadn't broken just the wooden base. It was the bowl. It had cracked into several pieces. I wrapped the package in some bunched sheets of *Stars and Stripes* and covered those with a layer of parcel paper. Then I took it to the airstrip. I followed Pete's orders to the letter, and I did not delay.

Really, now. Is the part about the bowl true? Did I do that?

No. Never. I would never deliberately take something

precious from a man – the pride of his collection, say, or his own pride – and put it under my foot like that, and twist my foot on it, and break it.

No. Not even for his own good.

I Right a Wrong

Sergeant Benet's tour ended a month before mine. They kept promising me a replacement but none came, because units up north had greater need. The day before his departure I was told I'd have to wait at least another week, which news I did not take well.

Sergeant Benet didn't want to go by helicopter to Saigon, he wanted to go by road. The road was worse, actuarially. His odds were better in the air, but of course he knew that as well as I did. This was just a feeling he had. We attached ourselves to an American convoy from Dong Tam and made the city late afternoon the day before Sergeant Benet's flight home. We were running behind time, but before dropping him off at out-processing I convinced him to stop on Tu Do Street for one last beer. I had some idea that we might have a personal talk. Instead we watched a Vietnamese girl in a white cowboy hat sing like Patsy Cline. The troops in the bar were actually listening to her. They were all white.

This was a cracker joint. I took some time figuring that out, being white myself, and by then we were attracting unfriendly attention. Nobody said anything, but they looked us over. I wouldn't have made much of it except for the way it affected Sergeant Benet. He sat low in his chair and drew into himself in a way that reduced his presence, offering self-diminishment as a peace bond. There was something timeworn and entirely dignified in his attitude, but I felt like a fool, and I wanted to say so. What I said was, "I hope you know how much you're going to miss me."

"Yes sir, I believe I will."

"I was joking."

"I know."

The girl was singing "Crazy." We went back to watching her.

For eleven months we had lived together. Each of those mornings Sergeant Benet had appeared in fresh fatigues, with our day already mapped out. He called me sir. He found work for us to do when there didn't seem to be any and somehow let me know what orders I should give him to preserve the fiction of my authority. I knew that he was my superior in every way that mattered, but he didn't allow me to acknowledge this and gave no sign of suspecting it himself. If he had, our barely sufficient imitation of purposeful existence would have collapsed. I understood all that. But I'd hoped to say some word of truth to him here at the end, to show some recognition of the facts. I didn't intend to flatter him, or even thank him. I just wanted him to know I wasn't stupid. And to accomplish this I had brought him to a redneck gutbucket.

Sergeant Benet finished his beer. "Time we hatted up," he said.

We drove the rest of the way in silence, according to our custom. When we reached out-processing Sergeant Benet let me carry his duffel bag inside the gate.

I set it down among some others. "I don't see how I can stay there alone," I said.

"You'll do just fine, sir."

"Forget I said that."

"They'll send somebody else down, for sure. You got, what, twenty-eight days?"

"Thirty."

"Thirty days. One at a time, sir, like the man says."

A second lieutenant came over and snapped his fingers for Sergeant Benet's orders. He began to read through them, and without looking up he said, "You're late."

I had rank on him. I could have locked his keels and smoked him good, but I kept quiet. Whatever I said now, Sergeant Benet would pay for later. He wasn't mine anymore.

It was too late to head back to My Tho, so I booked into a hotel near Cholon. There was a bar on the roof and a small malarial-looking pool and a bandstand where a knock-kneed girl in go-go boots was dancing to scratchy records and talking to the men watching her. From where I sat I looked across at a line of buildings ruined by the fighting at Tet, collapsed walls exposing furnished rooms like stage sets.

I drank brandy through what was left of the afternoon. This was not my habit. I began to feel lucid and strong. I thought of things I could have said and done to the men in the bar who had made Sergeant Benet agree to seem smaller than he was. At sunset I went to the railing and puked. I stood there as night came on, watching flares go up across the river. I could see tracers streaking back and forth near a distant bridge but the sound was lost in the clamor of the streets below. It seemed to me I made an interesting figure, staring out into the darkness with my pipe in my mouth. It was a Kaywoodie I'd bought at the PX to help me ease off cigarettes. The pipe, the idea of myself smoking a pipe, alone at the railing, gave me a gallant and philosophical picture of myself. I smoked my pipe and gazed over the city, over the people below, to whom I felt superior because I was feeling deep and dark things of which they were ignorant. This was when the idea came to me to go back to that cracker establishment. The thought of the place produced a sense of obligation, as if it was my duty to return and introduce these backward folk to the notion of consequence.

I didn't get there anytime soon. There were other venues in between. I turned up on another hotel rooftop, the Rex, arguing almost to the point of blows with a helicopter pilot about *Bonnie and Clyde*. He thought the violence was gratuitous. Then I was in a dive on a side street somewhere. Then another dive. Then the cracker joint. At a certain moment I became brightly conscious that I was there, though I had no memory of getting there from the last place I'd been. The night was without transitions.

An American was up on the stage, singing and pounding an acoustic guitar whose fancy inlays glittered in the lights. He had long stringy hair and a stringy, truly pathetic beard. All the crackers joined in when he got to the last line: "I'll never get out of this world alive!" They were actually stomping and slapping their knees.

"Why, you stupid cracker," I said to the fellow next to me at the bar. He had a long white face and thick glasses in owlish black frames. He cupped a hand at his ear and leaned over. "Beg pardon?"

"Stupid cracker!"

"Dusty!" He pointed at the singer and shook his head as if to say, Is this guy great or what?

I checked up and down the bar to see if anyone was looking at me so I could say, What the *fuck* are you looking at? Then I lit my pipe and leaned back and almost fell off my stool. My neighbor caught me by the arm. "Whoa," he said. "You don't look too hot there, fella."

"Can't breathe."

"What?"

"Can't breathe."

"You okay?"

I shook off his hand and made my way outside. I was in the alley out back, leaning against the wall, when fate sent me some customers. They came out of the bar and looked around and started to bicker. There was a tall guy with his arm in a cast up to his elbow, and two buckaroos wearing identical yellow shirts, with yokes and pearl buttons. Except for the shirts they didn't look anything alike. One had a big plume of red hair and simian arms that poked way out of his sleeves. The other was a trim fellow, small head, very neat-looking, neat in his movements, very pleased to have himself in such good order. He had a toothpick in his mouth. It bothered me that they would dress this way without being twins.

"Okay, we're here," the redheaded buckaroo said, "so where the hell is Henry?"

"He's coming," said the guy in the cast.

"He's supposed to be here. That was the deal."

160

"He'll be here. Just hold your horses."

I started singing "We Shall Overcome."

The two buckaroos talked about Henry, whether they should wait for him or not.

I sang louder. "We'll walk hand in ha-and, We'll walk hand in ha-and . . ."

They looked at me. The one in the cast said, "You got a problem?"

"I'm a Negro," I said.

The trim buckaroo took out his toothpick as if he meant to say something, then put it back in his mouth.

The guy in the cast said, "I guess you do have a problem at that."

"I ain't got all night," the redhead said.

"Me neither," the trim one said. "If Henry thinks he's got some kind of monopoly around here, he is sadly mistaken."

"That's it," the redhead said. "That is the whole truth."

"I'm a Negro," I said. "What're you stupid rednecks going to do about that?"

"I could kick your ass," the guy in the cast said. "Would that satisfy you?" He was sweating profusely. His shiny black skirt was streaked white with salt stains and his eyes bulged like a horse's.

The trim fellow turned to me and took out his toothpick. "Sleep it off, buddy," he said. "You're kind of getting in the way."

"I was here first," I said. "You're the one who's in the way, asshole."

I didn't see him swing. He came out of nowhere and nailed me right in the face. I felt something crack inside

161

my mouth. I have to say it discouraged me. The tall guy
stepped up and swung his cast like a bat. When I ducked
under it the redhead grabbed my arm and yanked it behind
my back. He slipped a headlock on me and tightened it up
to where I couldn't move without breaking my own neck.
Those chimpanzee arms of his were like cables. Then the
trim buckaroo hit me in the mouth again, and on the
ear, and over my eye. He stood there bopping my head
while his pal held me tight. He didn't have much power
in those neat little hands, but they were hard as nuts and
he kept them coming. I could hear the guy in the cast
laughing wildly. After a time the redhead asked me if I'd
had enough. I nodded. He let go and I bent over, hands
on my knees, trying to fill my lungs. When I straightened
up they were watching me. The guy in the cast was still
laughing. The other two were alert. I turned and walked
up the alley toward the street.

Even before I touched my head I felt the bumps coming
out. I turned the corner and stopped and checked myself
over. There were bumps on my forehead and on top of my
skull, under my hair. But it was my teeth that had me
worried. Something had broken in there and was floating
around my mouth. I spat it into my hand, a jagged black
thing. I studied it for a while. It was a chunk of the
mouthpiece of my Kaywoodie. Here was a lesson, some
profit for my pains. This was the last time I'd start a fight
with a pipe in my mouth.

Still, I hated to lose that pipe.

I turned and went back up the alley. When they saw me
coming they faced me and waited. "You want some more?"
the redhead asked.

I told him I was looking for my pipe.

They watched as I searched for it, patrolling the ground in a crouch, then on my hands and knees. And then they joined me, even the one in the cast. We were all on our hands and knees, feeling our way in the shadows, patting the damp stones. None of us spoke. After a while the redhead hollered, "Got it!" We gathered around him where he knelt. He turned the pipe over in his hand. "It's broke," he said sadly.

"Mouthpiece is broken," I said.

He handed me the pipe. "Still nice and shiny. Maybe they can fix it."

"It's got a guarantee," I said.

"Sure, just send it in," the trim one said.

The one in the cast said "Ha!" He said it with such bitterness that we all looked at him. "You'll never see the fucker again," he said. "They'll say the guarantee don't apply because you didn't do this or you didn't do that. Some technicality. Lying bastards!"

The redhead stood and brushed his hands. "So, I suppose you know all about it."

"I know. Believe me, I fucking know." He looked from one to the other of us. He was ready to go the distance on this.

"I don't believe Henry's coming at all," said the trim fellow.

Through the open door we could hear Dusty singing "El Paso." We fell silent and listened to him, right to the very end. One little kiss, and Felina, good-bye.

Souvenir

Our guns were deployed on the edge of a refugee camp. Some evidence remained of the old village the camp had swallowed – a big, breezy, tile-roofed house that used to belong to the local mandarin, and a few hooches of sturdy construction. The new quarters had been knocked together out of scrap lumber, flattened cans, cardboard, old tarps and ponchos. Open ditches carried sewage to the canal where the women did their laundry and their fishing. There were few men, and they were shy of being seen. These were people who had lost their homes during Tet.

The battalion had set up headquarters in the mandarin's house. I was sprawled on the steps, shirt off; baking in the sun. A yellow cat ran past, chased by a pack of kids. A spotter plane circled slowly in the distance.

Captain Kale clomped down the steps. Captain Kale was a newly arrived infantry officer waiting assignment to another battalion. They'd sent him over to assume my so-called responsibilities until an artillery officer could be found to replace me, which might take a while. Sergeant Benet's replacement, now off on a supply mission, had come in almost two weeks late.

Captain Kale was disappointed by this assignment. We

had just a few more days until I left, but there were times when I wondered if we'd make it. He was strongly of the opinion that I had failed in my duty. I'd babied the Vietnamese, he thought, instead of raising them to American standards of aggression. They lacked the killer spirit, and Captain Kale was bullish on the killer spirit.

He had a round glistening face as pink as a boiled ham. It was the face of a soft little man but in fact he was tall and bulging with muscles. In the odd moments when we were stalled somewhere, waiting for a ride, waiting for Major Chau, when the cognoscenti found some shade and lay back with their caps over their eyes, Captain Kale knocked out push-ups by the hundred. If there was a solid wall nearby he'd do isometrics. While he worked out he told me how he was going to turn his future battalion into a killer fighting unit, unlike this one, and how it was a good thing I was leaving the army, because if every officer were like me the VC would walk off with the whole country inside of a week. My silence did not discourage him. He regarded talking – "speaking his mind" – as a form of bravery, "and let the chips fall where they may."

Captain Kale owned records of people playing accordions, and could tell the difference between them. He had learned just enough Vietnamese to be able to issue peremptory orders that everyone ignored because it was pleasant to do so and because it was known that Major Chau, whom he had already unforgivably affronted, would tolerate such disobedience. He wore an Australian bush hat with little corks that swung from the brim in front of his eyes. In his spare time he ordered things from the catalog of a company in Singapore that sold cut-rate reproductions of

Bavarian artifacts – cuckoo clocks, furniture made from antlers, figurines in lederhosen, steins inscribed with folkish sayings. He intended to furnish his house with these goods. He'd seen them, he said, and there was no way you could tell they weren't German.

Captain Kale came down the steps and stopped beside me, blocking my sun. His face was awash in sweat. "What are you doing?" he said. "Are you doing something?"

"As you see."

"I need a sling," he said.

"A sling." I sat up. "And what do you need a sling for?"

"Division wants to move one of the guns. Don't ask me why, I've got negative intel. Nobody tells me squat."

"Where're they moving it?"

"Negative intel. They just said to get it ready. A Chinook's on the way."

"Lieutenant Nanh's the quartermaster. Next time you need some gear, talk to him."

"That's what I did. He said talk to Sergeant Tuy. Sergeant Tuy said talk to Lieutenant Nanh. If I get any more of this runaround I'm gonna start busting heads."

"Lieutenant Nanh has the slings."

"Then why didn't he goddamn say so?"

"Maybe you didn't ask him right. Maybe you didn't say the magic word."

"Maybe," he said, "you could find it in your heart to say the magic word for me."

"That's what I was planning to do." I buttoned my fatigue jacket and untied Canh Cho's leash from the railing. He raised his head and blinked. His coat was powdered with the red dust, fine as talc, that covered everything here. His tail thumped once on the step.

Captain Kale looked down at him. "This is no job for an American officer," he said. "Sweet-talking these people."

"You should put in for a translator."

"Yeah, sure. That's just what I need, a Cong spy taking down every word I say."

Lieutenant Nanh was sitting in his jeep, monitoring the radio. I asked him what was happening in the field. Nothing so far, he said. I said, The communists are afraid of us. He agreed with me. I told him a Chinook was coming for one of the guns and that we were going to need a sling. Of course, he said. He called a man over and told him to get a sling.

I asked him if Captain Kale had spoken to him.

Lieutenant Nanh shrugged and said, "Captain Kale." Just his name, as if that explained everything. Then he wagged his finger at Canh Cho and smacked his lips. The dog retreated the full length of the leash, trembling violently.

When I got back with the sling Captain Kale was trying to couple the howitzer to a truck, yelling orders at the driver: Forward! Back! Left! Right! Clearly, it was no easy thing to execute precise rearward maneuvers in a two-and-a-half-ton truck, under the guidance of a red-faced giant whose every word sounded like a curse; but it was also clear that the driver was not doing his best. *Au contraire,* he was staging a farce for his friends on the gun crews, who cheered him on as he jockeyed the truck to and fro, sometimes teasingly close to the hitch but always just out of reach. "Stop!" Captain Kale shouted. The driver sawed the wheel, raising more dust. "Stop! Stop!"

Finally the driver took the truck out of gear and faced

167

Captain Kale with a look of calculated stupidity. "That's enough," I told him in Vietnamese. "I'll take over."

The driver climbed down from the cab, bowing at the applause.

Captain Kale walked up to me. "What did you tell that man?"

"I think I'd better drive."

"Did you tell him to quit?"

"He seemed to be having some problems understanding you."

"I said, did you tell him to quit?"

"Yes sir."

"He was under my orders. Not your orders – my orders!"

"Yes sir."

"That Chinook is going to be here any minute now, and this gun's going to be ready for it."

"Yes sir. I'll drive."

"No! You'll fuck up. I'll drive. You hitch the gun."

We accomplished this without difficulty. Then Captain Kale drove the howitzer out of its emplacement and over to the courtyard of the mandarin's house, where he stopped and turned off the engine. The courtyard was still open in the middle, but a ring of hooches had encroached on the periphery. I walked up as the crew began to unhitch the gun. "Wait," I said. They stopped what they were doing. Before Captain Kale could say anything, I told him we needed more space.

"Horse manure. There's plenty of room. It's not going to land, it's just going to grab the gun and go."

"These hooches are too close."

"So where else is there?"

"There's that field by the canal."

"Too swampy."

"We could try."

"Truck'll get bogged down. Then I'm really in dutch."

"Okay then, the road. We can drive out of town a little ways and do it there."

"No time for that. Chopper's on the way."

"They'll wait. What'll it take, another twenty minutes?"

"No time, like I said. I was told to have this gun ready, and it's goddamn going to be ready." He ordered the crew to finish unhitching the howitzer.

"You haven't actually done this before," I said.

"Bet your ass I have."

"Not really."

"Have too."

"When?"

"You are fucking with my shit, Lieutenant. I will not have my shit fucked with."

When the gun was free Captain Kale had the truck driven away while he attached the sling. Then he popped a smoke grenade. Women and kids gathered in front of the hooches to watch. They knew they were in for some kind of show. Captain Kale should've had them moved out, he should've had the whole area cleared, but I didn't tell him that. Nor did I offer him the ski goggles in my pack. I just stood there with the others and watched.

The gun crew heard it first. They straightened up and stared into the sky, hands above their eyes. Then I heard it, a faint thwacking in the air. A few moments later the Chinook came into view, flying in high from the east. It followed the canal up to the village, then banked into a

169

slow circle overhead, huge even at this height, huge and improbable.

"Lieutenant?" Captain Kale said. "Yoo-hoo, Lieutenant? Do you think you could handle the radio? If you're not too busy? Do you think you could do that without totally fucking up?"

Our radio operator had set up shop on the edge of the courtyard. I squatted beside him and dialed up the air support frequency. The pilot was already giving our call sign. I answered him, and he asked if that was our smoke he was seeing. That's it, I told him. You're right above it. He asked if I was sure I wanted him to come in there. That's what the boss wants, I said. The pilot said it looked a little tight, but he could do it, if that was the deal.

This was the way out. I could have called the Chinook off, asked him to come back in twenty minutes, then told Captain Kale that the pilot wouldn't come in so close and we'd have to go to the road. That's what I should have done, but I didn't think of it, and the reason I didn't think of it was that I wanted Captain Kale's will to be entirely fulfilled. I wanted his orders followed to the letter, without emendation or abridgment, so that whatever happened got marked to his account, and to his account alone. I wanted this thing to play itself out to the end. I was burning, I wanted it so much.

"That's what he wants," I said.

The Chinook made several spirals, dropping fast, then leveled off and began to lower itself more slowly, even gingerly, as if by inches, its vast drab belly growing laboriously more vast, eclipsing the sun, the sun backlighting a fiery line around the body and glinting in the blur of the rotors.

The shadow overspread the ground, fell over every upturned face. The great rotors beat the air, pounding hypnotically, ardently, like the sound of a heart through a stethoscope. The thatch on the rooftops started to rustle. I put my hand to my cap. The women claimed their children and pulled them out of the yard. Their hair blew in the stiffening downdraft. Dust swirled around them. They backed away coughing, waving their hands in front of their faces. The Chinook lurched downward, caught itself, then resumed its measured descent.

The center of the courtyard was deserted except for Captain Kale, who stood atop the howitzer with the sling noose in his hands. I could barely see him through the thickening storm of dust. The Chinook was maybe thirty feet overhead, letting itself down in a series of short drops and checks. The rotors whipped the air down and whipped it down again as it rushed upward off the ground. It grew wild, furious, a chaos of winds. A man ran out of a hooch with a small child under one arm. Then, as if they'd been waiting for a signal, people were boiling out of the doorways, shouting, stumbling, some half dressed, carrying babies and boxes and bags. Canh Cho started howling. The thatch lifted on the hooches, snapping back and forth, straining, tearing loose, whirling in the eddies. The air was full of it. A sheet of tin flapped on a wall, broke off, banged away over the ground. A big piece of plywood went flying. I heard a hooch collapse across the yard. The Chinook was suspended above the howitzer, the hook swinging from its belly. Captain Kale raised the noose above his head. The hook was just out of reach. He lifted the noose higher and made a lunge but missed, and the Chinook rose a few feet and held on there, pounding, pounding, pounding. Another hooch crashed down. Then, almost in the same instant, another. They were coming apart. The junk they'd been made of was blowing all over the yard. The Chinook inched down again. Captain Kale reached up with the noose. The hook was just above him. He couldn't miss. He missed. He missed again. The dust had blinded him, for sure. I got up and started toward him, but just then he made another pass at the hook and caught it and jumped off the gun. His knees buckled and he fell hard. The Chinook eased upward, cables creaking as they tightened around the howitzer. The barrel tipped down, then rocked back as the gun lifted free. The Chinook beat its way up. I shielded my eyes against the churning dust. I heard a loud crack somewhere, the whump of the blades, Canh Cho wailing. He hadn't stopped since he started. The Chinook rose steadily, the gun swinging below it, then made a lumbering turn and chopped back eastward above the canal.

I watched until I couldn't hear it anymore.

The courtyard was still. The air had an ochre tint. I looked around at what had been done here. This was my work, this desolation had blown straight from my own heart. I marked the discovery coolly, as if for future study. This was, I understood, something to be remembered, though I had no idea what that would mean. I couldn't guess how the memory would live on in me, shadowing my sense of entitlement to an inviolable home; touching me, years hence, in my own home, with the certainty that some terrible wing is even now descending, bringing justice.

I suspected none of this. I felt regret, but even more surprise.

Captain Kale was limping in little circles, talking to himself and rubbing angrily at his eyes. He looked demented. As I came toward him I told him to stop rubbing, that he was only making it worse. He stood there with his fingers spread out in front of his face, blinking hard. I screwed the lid off my canteen and held it out to him. He seized it and tilted his head back and let the water pour into his open eyes. It ran down his cheeks and neck and under his collar, washing pale streaks in the dust that caked his skin. His uniform was red with the stuff. He took a mouthful of water, spit it out, took another, and looked around. His eyes were swollen almost shut. "My God," he said.

"It's a mess, all right."

He handed me the canteen. "It's like a bomb went off."

"Not really," I said. "A bomb is something else again."

He didn't answer. He was staring around at the women in the courtyard, watching them shuffle through the debris on the ground. They seemed to know which piece of wood was theirs, which scrap of tin. There was no quarreling among them. I noticed an unframed picture lying a little ways off. I walked over and picked it up. A picture of a girl. Stiff paper with scalloped edges, yellow with age. Captain Kale asked to see it. I blew off the dust and handed it to him. We both studied it. A sepia portrait of a teenage girl in white ao dai, sitting erect before a painted backdrop of hanging vines with a crescent moon shining through. Her hands were in her lap. Her expression was grave and dreamy.

"She must be one of these mama-sans," I said.

He looked up at the women moving around us. "You think she's one of *them*?"

"I imagine so."

Captain Kale carried the picture over to one of the women and held it out to her, but she wouldn't look at it. When he touched her arm she pulled away and went on with her work. He offered the picture to another woman and she wouldn't look at it either. None of them would. Someday it would end up in his Bavarian trophy case, with his Chicom rifle and VC flag and all the medals he was going to write himself up for, but Captain Kale didn't know that yet. He was new here. He went from woman to woman, begging them to examine the picture, holding it out as if it proved something important. His voice was cracked, he sounded close to tears, but they were deaf and blind to him. They wouldn't look, they wouldn't listen, and they couldn't have understood him anyway. He was speaking English.

The Rough Humor of Soldiers

My last night in My Tho. The battalion officers were giving me a farewell party. We began the evening at a bar in town, then moved on to Major Chau's house for dinner. Madame Chau was nowhere in evidence, nor were any of their children. When we'd all assembled and settled ourselves in a circle on the floor Major Chau rang a bell and a young woman entered the room. She was made up heavily, even ceremonially, her face whitened, her cheeks rouged, her lips painted red. Her perfume was thick and sweet. Major Chau introduced the young woman as his niece, Miss Bep. She bowed, then took a tray filled with brandy glasses from the sideboard and moved around the circle of men, bending before each of us with downcast eyes. Captain Kale took his glass and thanked her and she moved on to me without a word, but in passing looked back at him and gave him what might have been a smile; it was gone too soon to say. The face she presented to me was impeccably bland.

Then she came around with a large bottle of Martell and filled our glasses. Again she looked at Captain Kale, and again, unmistakably this time, smiled.

175

"What's your secret?" I asked him.

"Knock it off," he said.

Captain Kale had a wife to whom he intended to be true.

Miss Bep returned the bottle to the sideboard and took the empty place to Major Chau's right. This was the first time in my experience that a woman had joined a circle of officers rather than serving and leaving. Captain Kale was watching her with a rude, unconscious fixity. No one took any notice. The room was blue with smoke, loud with boasts and insults. Pots banged in the kitchen.

We emptied our glasses and Miss Bep went around again with the Martell. She gave more to Captain Kale than to anyone else. When she resumed her place beside Major Chau she turned and whispered in his ear.

Major Chau leaned forward. "My niece says the American captain is very handsome."

Captain Kale shifted, shifted again. The lotus position was torture to those pumped-up haunches. There were wet patches on the back of his shirt, widening rings under his arms. His pink face shone. "Please convey my compliments to Miss Bep on her extremely nice looks," he said, and nodded at her. "Miss Bep is very beautiful."

The other officers whistled and slapped their knees when Major Chau translated this. Miss Bep spoke into his ear again.

"My niece says the American captain looks like the great Fred Astaire."

Miss Bep said something else to Major Chau.

"My niece asks, Has the great Astaire found his Ginger Rogers here in My Tho?"

176

"No," Captain Kale said in Vietnamese.

Major Chau got up and went over to the stereo Sergeant Benet and I had bought him at the PX. He put on Brenda Lee's "I'm Sorry" and motioned for Captain Kale to rise. "My niece would be honored to dance with the great Astaire," he said.

"I'm not that great," he said, but he stood and walked over to Miss Bep. He held out his hand. She took it and rose lightly and without hesitation moved into his arms. They danced in the center of our circle, swaying to the music, hardly moving their feet at all. At first she looked up at him, then slowly let her head fall forward against his chest. Her eyes were closed. I could see the play of her fingers on the back of his neck.

Then Captain Kale closed his eyes too, and his face became gentle and calm. He was transfigured. The Vietnamese officers were watching him with peculiar concentration. Major Chau rolled his shoulders to the music, mouthing words as he stacked more 45s on the turntable:

> *They tell me*
> *Mistakes*
> *Are part of bein' young*
> *But that don't right*
> *The wrong that's been done . . .*

After the song ended, Captain Kale and Miss Bep went on swaying together to their own music, then roused themselves and stepped groggily apart, her hand still in his. The officers called out encouragement. I joined in, though I was nearly deranged with envy and incomprehension.

177

A record fell, the needle hissed, Connie Francis began to sing.

Evening shadows make me blue
When each weary day is through

"You need more room," Major Chau said. "In here is too many peoples. Come." He beckoned to Captain Kale and gestured toward the doorway leading to the back of the house. "Come!" Captain Kale looked at him, looked at Miss Bep. They were still holding hands. She gave him that ghostly smile, then led him out of the circle and through the doorway behind Major Chau. The major returned, took his place, and rang the bell again. A pair of old women carried in trays from the kitchen.

· While we filled our plates Major Chau raised his glass and began reciting a toast to me. He praised my implacable enmity toward the communist insurgents, my skill as a leader of men, my reckless courage under fire. He said that my presence here had dealt the Vietcong a blow they'd never recover from. Through all this Major Chau maintained an air of utmost gravity, and so did the other officers. When he was done the adjutant proposed a toast even more elevated. They were all stuffing themselves now, except the adjutant and, of course, me. That was part of the prank. As long as I was being toasted I had to sit there and listen with an expression of humility and gratitude. Lieutenant Nanh spoke next. Then another officer stepped in.

I was hungry. Somewhere in the back of the house

178

Captain Kale was slow-dancing with Miss Bep. The toasts went on.

I'd expected something like this, but I didn't know what a nuisance it would be to sit through. Behind the understanding that all this was a joke, we had another understanding that it was not a joke at all, that in my time here I had succeeded only in staying alive. Their satiric praise created by implication a picture of me that was also a picture of what I feared. I had become, a man in hiding.

At last they stopped and let me eat. Spring rolls, clear soup, fish and rice, noodles stirred up with shoots and greens and cubes of tender meat. "Where's This Place Called Lonely Street?" was on the record player. I'd just about finished my first helping when I heard a yell from the back of the house. The officers sat up, searched one another out with swift glances. Silence. Then another yell – a roar, really – and the sound of Captain Kale coming our way. He stomped into the room and stood there, staring at me, his face bleached white. His mouth was smeared with lipstick. He held his hands clenched in front of him like a runner frozen in midstride. I looked at him, he looked at me. Then Lieutenant Nanh made a sobbing sound and buried his face in his hands and fell sideways onto the floor. He kicked his foot out like a ham playing a dying man and knocked over a bowl of rice. Major Chau let off a series of shrill hoots – *whoo whoo whoo* – and then they all doubled over. They were wailing and shrieking and pounding the floor. Captain Kale gave no sign that he heard them.

"Did you know she was a guy?" he said.

I was too surprised to speak. I shook my head.

179

He gave me his full attention. Then he said, "I'd kill you if you did."

I understood that he meant it. Another close call.

Captain Kale looked at the others as if they'd just materialized in the room. He walked around them and out the door. After I heard the jeep start up and drive away I couldn't keep from treating myself to a few laughs while I ate my dinner. The officers kept trying to pull themselves together, but every time they looked at me they blew a gasket. At first I played along like a sport, thinking they'd lose interest, but they'd entered a state where anything I did – spearing my food, lifting my fork, chewing – set them off again. Finally Lieutenant Nanh managed to sit up and catch his breath. He watched me fill my plate yet again with noodles and diced meat. "*Bon appetit*," he said.

"This is good," I said. "What is it?"

He pitched over onto his back and let out a howl. He lay there, drumming his feet and panting soundlessly. I looked down at my plate. "Oh no," I said. "You didn't do that."

But of course that was exactly what they'd done. What else could I expect? What else could *he* expect, with a name like Dog Stew? That pooch was up against some very strong karma, far beyond the power of my stopgap, sentimental intercessions. In moments of clarity I'd known he would come to this. He knew it himself in his doggy way, and the knowledge had given him a morose, dull, hopeless cast of mind. He bore his life like a weight, yet trembled to lose it. I'd been fretting about his prospects. Now my worries were over. So were his. At least there was some largesse in this conclusion, some reciprocity. I had fed him, now he fed me, and fed me, I have to say, right tastily.

There was only one way left to do him justice. I bent to my plate and polished him off.

PART THREE

Civilian

I was discharged in Oakland the day after I stepped off the plane. The personnel officer asked me if I would consider signing up for another tour. I could go back as a captain, he said. Captain? I said. Captain of *what*?

He didn't try to argue with me, just made me watch him take his sweet time fiddling with the file folders on his desk before handing over my walking papers and separation pay. I went back to the bachelor officers quarters and paced my room, completely at a loss. For the first time in four years I was absolutely free to follow my own plan. The trouble was, I didn't have one. When the housekeeping detail asked me to leave I packed up and caught a taxi to San Francisco.

For over a week I stayed at a hotel in the Tenderloin, hitting the bars, sleeping late, and wandering the city, sharply aware that I was no longer a soldier and feeling that change not the way I'd imagined, as freedom and pleasure, but as aimlessness and solitude. It wasn't that I missed the army. I didn't. But I'd been a soldier since I was eighteen, not a good soldier but a soldier, and linked by that fact to other soldiers, even those long dead. When, browsing through a bookstore, I came across a collection of letters sent home by Southern troops during the Civil War, I heard their voices as those of men I'd known. Now I was nothing in particular and joined to no one.

In the afternoons I put myself through forced marches down to the wharf, through Golden Gate Park, out to the Cliff House. I walked around the Haight, seedier than a year before, afflicted like the faces on the street with a trashed, sullen quality. Sniffling guys in big overcoats hunched in doorways, hissing at passersby, though not at me: a clue that I was radiating some signal weirdness of my own. No hug patrols in evidence. I went there once and didn't go back.

As I walked I kept surprising myself in the windows I passed, a gaunt hollow-eyed figure in button-down shirt and khakis and one of my boxy Hong Kong sport coats. Without cap or helmet my head seemed naked and oversized. I looked newly hatched, bewildered, without history.

There might have been some affectation in this self-imposed quarantine. I didn't have to stay in a seedy room in San Francisco, broodingly alone; I could have gone on to Washington. My mother and brother gave every sign of wanting to welcome me home, and so did my friends, and Vera. She had parted ways with Leland soon after they took up together, and her most recent letters had spoken of her wish to try again with me. All I had to do was get on a plane and within hours I would be surrounded by the very people I'd been afraid of not seeing again. But I stayed put.

I thought of my friends and family as a circle, and this was exactly the picture that stopped me cold and kept me where I was. It didn't seem possible to stand in the center of that circle. I did not feel equal to it. I felt morally embarrassed. Why this was so I couldn't have said, but a sense of deficiency, even blight, had taken hold of me. In Vietnam I'd barely noticed it, but here, among people who did not take corruption and brutality for granted, I came to understand that I did, and that this set me apart. San Francisco was an open, amiable town, but I had trouble holding up my end of a conversation. I said horrifying things without knowing it until I saw the reaction. My laugh sounded bitter and derisive even to me. When people asked me the simplest questions about myself I became cool and remote. Lonesome as I was, I made damn sure I stayed that way.

One day I took a bus over to Berkeley. I had the idea of applying for school there in the fall and it occurred to me I might get a break on admission and fees because of my father being a California resident. It wasn't easy to collect hard intelligence about the old man, but since the state had kept him under lock and key for over two years, and on parole ever since, I figured his home of record was one thing we could all agree on.

I never made it to the admissions office. There was some sort of gathering in Sproul Plaza, and I stopped to listen to one speaker and then another. Though it was sunny I got cold in the stiff bay breeze and sat down by a hedge. The second speaker started reading a list of demands addressed to President Johnson. People were walking around, eating, throwing Frisbees for dogs with handkerchiefs around their necks. On a blanket next to me a bearded guy and a languorous Chinese girl were passing a joint back and forth. The girl was very beautiful.

Microphone feedback kept blaring out the speaker's

words, but I got the outline. Withdrawal of our troops from Vietnam. Recognition of Cuba. Immediate commutation of student loans. Until all these demands were met, the speaker said he considered himself in a state of unconditional war with the United States government.

I laughed out loud.

The bearded guy on the blanket gave me a look. He said something to the Chinese girl, who turned and peered at me over the top of her sunglasses, then settled back on her elbows. I asked him what he thought was so interesting and he said something curt and dismissive and I didn't like it, didn't like this notion of his that he could scrutinize me and make a judgment and then brush me off as if I didn't exist. I said a few words calculated to let him know that he would be done with me when I was done with him, and then he stood up and I stood up. His beautiful girlfriend pulled on his hand. He ignored her. His mouth was moving in his beard. I hardly knew what he was saying, but I understood his tone perfectly and it was intolerable to me. I answered him. I could hear the rage in my voice and it pleased me and enraged me still more. I gave no thought to my words, just said whatever came to me. I hated him. If at that moment I could have turned his heart off, I would have. Then I saw that he had gone quiet. He stood there looking at me. I heard the crazy things I was saying and realized, even as I continued to yell at him, that he was much younger than I'd thought, a boy with ruddy cheeks his beard was too sparse to hide. When I managed to stop myself I saw that the people around us were watching me as if I were pitiful. I turned away and walked toward Sather Gate, my face burning.

•   •   •

I got to Manhattan Beach just after sundown and surprised my father once again. He was in his bathrobe, about to pop some frozen horror into the oven. I told him to keep it on ice and let me stand him to dinner at the restaurant where we'd eaten the year before. He said he wasn't feeling exactly jake, thought he might be coming down with something, but after we had a few drinks he let himself be persuaded of the tonic potential of a night on the town.

So we gave it another try, and this time we got it right. Again we stuffed ourselves with meat and drink, and again my father grew immense with pleasure and extended his benevolence to everyone in range. The old rich rumble entered his voice; the stories began, stories of his youth and the companions of his youth, rioters whose deeds succeeded in his telling to the scale of legend. He found occasion to invoke the sacred names (Deerfield; New Haven; Bones; the Racquet Club), but this time I managed to get past the lyrics and hear his music, a formal yet droll music in which even his genuine pretensions sounded parodic. I asked no questions about Hadassah. I let him roll. In fact I egged him on. I didn't have to believe him; it was enough to look across the table and see him there, swinging to his own beat.

I had come back to Manhattan Beach, I surely understood even then, because there could no longer be any question of judgment between my father and me. He'd lost his claim to the high ground, and so had I. We could take each other now without any obligation to approve or disapprove or model our virtues. It was freedom, and we both grabbed at it. It was the best night we'd ever had.

I paid the next morning. So did he, and then some.

Late into the day he was still in bed, flushed and hot, and I finally realized that he really had been coming down with something. I called his doctor, who stopped by the apartment on his way home that evening, diagnosed the flu, and prescribed something to bring the fever down. He wouldn't let me pay, not after my father sneaked it in that I was just back from Vietnam. I followed the doctor to the door, insisting, wagging my wallet, but he wouldn't hear of it. When he left I went back to the old man's bedroom and found him laughing, and then I started laughing too. Couple of crooks.

That night and the next day he was too sick to do much of anything but sleep. In his sleep he moaned and talked to himself. I came into his room now and then and stood over him in the dim slatted light cast by the streetlamp. Big as he was, he looked as if he'd been toppled, felled. He slept like a child, knees drawn up almost to his chest. Sometimes he whimpered. Sometimes he put his thumb in his mouth. When I saw him like that he seemed much older than his sixty years, closer to the end and more alone than I wanted to think about.

Then he started coming out of it. He liked being babied, so he wore his invalid droop and mopery as long as I let him. When I helped him in and out of bed he groaned and mewed and walked as if his joints had rusted shut. He had me buy him an ice bag, which he wore like a tam-o'-shanter, his eyes tremulous with self-pity. All day long he called out his wishes in a small desolate voice – cheese and crackers, please, some Gouda on stone-ground Wheat Thins would be swell, with a little Tabasco and red onion, if I wouldn't mind. Palm hearts with cream cheese, *por favor*, and this

190

time could I skip the paprika and just sprinkle a little onion salt on them? Thanks a mil! Ginger ale, old son, over ice, and would it be too much trouble to *crush* the ice?

He was relentless and without shame. Once he pushed me too far and I said, "Jesus, Duke, suffer in silence awhile, okay?" This was the first time in my life I'd called him by that name, and the sound of myself saying it made me cringe. But he didn't object. It probably reassured him that I was ready to vacate any outstanding claims on him as his child and accept a position as his crony. I never called him Duke again. I wanted to feel as if I still had a father out there, however singular the terms.

He started feeling better after the second day, and I was almost sorry. I liked taking care of him. I'd blitzed the apartment with cleansers, stocked his cabinets with cans of stew and hash and clam chowder and the treats he favored – Swedish flatbread, palm hearts, macadamia nuts. I had a new muffler put on the Cadillac. While he was laid up sick the smallest acts felt purposeful and worthwhile, and freed me from the sodden sensation of uselessness. Out running errands, I found myself taking pleasure in the salt smell and hard coastal light, the way the light fired the red-tiled roofs and cast clean-edged shadows as black as tar. In the afternoons I brought a chair and a book out to the sidewalk and faced the declining sun, chest bared to the warmth, half listening for the old man's voice through the open window at my back. I was reading *Portnoy's Complaint*. Geoffrey had sent it to me some time before and I'd never been able to get past the first few pages, but now it came to life for me. I read it in a state of near collapse, tears spilling down my cheeks. It was the first thing I'd finished in months.

My father took note of my absorption. He wanted to know what was so fascinating. I let him have it when I was through, and that evening he told me he'd never read anything so disgusting – not that he'd finished it. Come on, I said. He had to admit it was funny. Funny! How could such a thing be funny? He was baffled by the suggestion.

"Okay," I said. "What do you think *is* funny, then?"

"What b-book, you mean?"

"Book. Movie. Whatever."

He looked at me suspiciously. He was stretched out on the couch, eating a plate of scrambled eggs. "*Wind in the Willows*," he said. Now there was a book that showed you didn't have to be dirty to be humorous. He happened to have a copy on hand and would be willing to prove his point.

More than willing; I knew he was dying to read it aloud. He'd done this before, to Geoffrey and me, one night in La Jolla seven years earlier. It was a dim memory, pleasant and rare in that it held the three of us together. Of the book itself I recalled nothing except an atmosphere of treacly Englishness. But I couldn't say no.

He started to read, smiling rhapsodically, the ice bag on his head. I was bored stiff until Toad of Toad Hall made his entrance and began his ruinous love affair with the automobile. "What dust clouds shall spring up behind me as I speed on my reckless way!" he cried. "What carts shall I fling carelessly into the ditch in the wake of my magnificent onset!" Toad had my attention. I found him funny, yes, but also familiar in a way that put me on alert.

Toad is arrested for stealing a car, and in the absence of any remorse is sentenced to twenty years in a dungeon.

He escapes dressed as a washerwoman and manages to commandeer the very car he was imprisoned for stealing, after the owner offers a lift to what he thinks is a weary old crone. Toad pins the Samaritan with an elbow and seizes the wheel. "Washerwoman indeed!" he shouts. "Ho, ho! I am the Toad, the motor-car snatcher, the prison-breaker, the Toad who always escapes! Sit still, and you shall know what driving really is, for you are in the hands of the famous, the skillful, the entirely fearless Toad!"

By now I knew where the déjà vu came from. My father was Toad. He wasn't playing Toad, he *was* Toad, and not only Toad the audacious, Toad the shameless and incorrigible, but, as the story gave occasion, good-hearted Toad, hospitable Toad, Toad for whom his friends would risk their very lives. I'd never seen my father so forgetful of himself, so undefended, so confiding.

He read the whole book. It took hours. I got up now and then to grab a beer and refill his glass of ginger ale, stretch, fix a plate of crackers and cheese, but quietly, so he wouldn't break stride. The night deepened around us. Cars stopped going by. We were entirely at home, alone in an island of lamplight. I didn't want anything to change.

But Toad couldn't keep up the pace. The hounds of respectability were on his neck, and finally they brought him down. He had no choice but to make a good act of contrition and promise to keep the peace, live within his means, be good.

My father closed the book. He put it down and looked over at me, shaking his head at this transparent subterfuge. He wasn't fooled. He knew exactly what Toad's promise was worth.

•   •   •

I'd meant only to touch down in Manhattan Beach, but day followed day and I was still there. In the afternoons I sat by the water and read. At night I went to a bar down the road, then came home and sat up with the old man, listening to music and shooting the breeze. We talked about everything except Vietnam and prison. Only once did he mention his life there, when I asked about a livid scar on his wrist. He told me he'd been cut in a fight over which television program to watch, and that stupid as it sounded he'd had no choice, and didn't regret it. I never heard him mention another inmate, never heard him say "the joint" or even "Chino." He gave the impression it hadn't touched him.

I was drinking too much. One night he asked me if I didn't want to give the old noggin a breather, and I stalked out and came back even drunker than usual. I wanted it understood that he could expect nothing of me, as I expected nothing of him. He didn't bring it up again. He seemed to accept the arrangement, and I found it congenial enough that I could even imagine going on in this way, the two of us in our own circle, living on our own terms. I had nearly six thousand dollars in the bank, a year's worth of unspent salary and hazardous duty pay. If I enrolled in the local community college I could milk another three hundred a month from the G.I. Bill. They didn't check to see if you actually went to class – all you had to do was sign up. I could get a place of my own nearby. Start writing. By the time my savings and subsidies ran out, I'd have a novel done. Just a thought, but it kept coming. I mentioned it to the old man. He seemed to like the idea.

It was a bad idea, conceived in laziness and certain to

end miserably for both of us. Instead of masquerading as a student I needed to *be* a student, because I was uneducated and lacked the discipline to educate myself. Same with the novel. The novel wouldn't get written, the money would all get spent, and then what? I had intimations of the folly of this plan, though I persisted in thinking about it.

I'd been in town about a week when I met a woman on the beach. She was reading and I was reading, so it seemed natural to compare notes. Her name was Jan. She did speech therapy in the local schools. She had four or five years on me, maybe more. Her nose was very long and thin and she wore her blond hair mannishly close. She was calm, easy to talk to, but when I asked her out she frowned and looked away. She picked up a handful of sand, let it run through her fingers. "All right," she said.

Grand Illusion was showing at the local art theater. We got there early and strolled to the end of the street and back until they opened the doors. Jan wore a white dress that rustled as she walked and made her skin look dark as chocolate. She had the coolness and serenity of someone who has just finished a long swim. As we were going inside I noticed that her zipper had slipped a few inches. Hold on, I said, and slowly pulled it up again, standing close behind her, my nose almost in her hair.

I had seen *Grand Illusion* before, many times. My friend Laudie and I had memorized Pierre Fresnay's death scene with Erich von Stroheim and used to play it out to impress our dates. But that night I couldn't even follow the plot, I was so conscious of this woman beside me, her scent, the touch of her shoulder against mine, the play of light on her bare arms. At last I figured do or die and took her hand. She

195

didn't pull away. A little while later she laced her fingers through mine.

When the lights came on I was awkward and so was she. We agreed to stop somewhere for a drink. She didn't have anyplace in mind so I took her to the bar where I'd been going, an alleged discotheque frequented by former servicemen and some still in uniform. The moment I saw Jan inside the place, in her white dress and cool, manifest sanity, I saw it for what it was – a hole. But she claimed she liked it and insisted on staying.

We'd just gotten our drinks when a hand fell on my shoulder.

"Hey, Cap'n, you trying to keep this lovely lady all to yourself? No fuckin way, man."

Dicky. Dicky and his sidekick, Sleepy.

Chairs scraped. Lighters and cigarettes and glasses descended on the table, a pitcher of beer. They were with us. Jan kept trying not to stare at Dicky, and kept failing. Dicky was clean-shaven but he had a big curly mustache tattooed above his lip. I couldn't tell whether his intention was serious or jocular, if he actually thought he resembled a person with a mustache or was just riffing on the idea. He claimed to have been with a marine recon team near the DMZ, even to have operated in North Vietnam. I didn't know what Sleepy's story was.

They were there every night, hopping tables. The last time I'd seen them they were trying to break into Sleepy's car after he'd locked the keys inside. Dicky rigged up a wire of some kind and when that didn't work right away he went into a rage and smashed out the driver's window, but not before he'd kicked some dents into the door panel and broken off the radio antenna. Sleepy stood there with the rest of us who'd come out of the bar to watch, and didn't say a word.

Dicky caught Jan looking at him. He looked back at her. "So," he said, "how'd you get to know this cabron? Hey, just kidding, the cap'n here's numero fuckin uno."

I told him we'd been to see a film together.

"*Film?* You saw a *film?* What happen, your specs get dirty? Hey, Sleepy, you hear that? The cap'n says he saw a film, I say, What happen, your specs get dirty?"

"I laughed," Sleepy said, "didn't you hear me laugh?"

"No, I didn't hear you laugh. Speak up, asshole! So what film did you see, Cap'n?" For some reason sweat was pouring out of his hair and down his face.

I gave Dicky the short description of *Grand Illusion*.

He was interested. "That was some bad shit, man, Whirl War One. All that bob wire and overcoats and shit, livin like a buncha moles, come out, take a look around, *eeeeeeeerrr, boom*, your fuckin head gets blown off. No way, man. No fuckin way. I couldn't get behind that shit *at all*. I mean, millions of assholes going south, right? Millions! It's like you take the whole city of L.A., tell em, Hey, muchachos, here's the deal, you just run into that bob wire over there and let those other fuckers put holes in you. Big Bertha, man. And poison gas, what about that mustard shit, you think you could handle that?"

Jan had her eyes on me. "Were you a captain?"

I'd told her I'd just come back from Vietnam, but nothing else. I shook my head no.

"But I tell you straight," Dicky said, "no bullshit. If they'd of had me and my team back in Whirl War One we coulda turned that shit around *real* fast. When Heinrich starts waking up in the morning with Fritzy's dick in his hand, maybe they decide to do their yodeling and shit at home, leave these other people the fuck alone, you hear what I'm saying?"

Sleepy's chin was on his chest. He said, "I hear you, man."

"What were you, then?" Jan said to me.

"First lieutenant."

"Same thing," Dicky said. "Lieutenant, cap'n, all the same – hang you out to dry every fuckin one of em."

"That's not true."

"The fuck it isn't. Fuckin officers, man."

"I didn't hang anybody out to dry. Except maybe another officer," I said. "A captain, as a matter of fact."

Dicky ran a napkin over his wet face and looked at it, then at me. Jan was also looking at me.

As soon as I started the story I knew I shouldn't tell it. It was the story about Captain Kale wanting to bring the Chinook into the middle of the hooches, and me letting him do it. I couldn't find the right tone. My first instinct was to make it somber and regretful, to show how much more compassionate I was than the person who had done this thing, how far I had evolved in wisdom since then, but it came off sounding phony. I shifted to a clinical, deadpan exposition. This proved even less convincing than the first pose, which at least acknowledged that the narrator had a stake in his narrative. The neutral tone was a lie, also a bore.

How do you tell such a terrible story? Maybe such a story shouldn't be told at all. Yet finally it will be told. But as soon as you open your mouth you have problems, problems of recollection, problems of tone, ethical problems. How can you judge the man you were now that you've escaped his circumstances, his fears and desires, now that you hardly remember who he was? And how can you honestly avoid judging him? But isn't there, in the very act of confession, an obscene self-congratulation for the virtue required to see your mistake and own up to it? And isn't it just like an American boy, to want you to admire his sorrow at tearing other people's houses apart? And in the end who gives a damn, who's listening? What do you owe the listener, and which listener do you owe?

As it happened, Dicky took the last problem out of my hands by laughing darkly when I confessed that I'd omitted to offer Captain Kale my ski goggles. He grinned at me, I grinned at him. Jan looked back and forth between us. We had in that moment become a duet, Dicky and I, and she was in the dark. She had no feel for what was coming, but he did, very acutely, and his way of encouraging me was to show hilarity at every promissory detail of the disaster he saw taking shape. He was with me, even a little ahead of me, and I naturally pitched my tune to his particular receptivities, which were harsh and perverse and altogether familiar, so that even as he anticipated me I anticipated him and kept him laughing and edgy with expectation.

And so I urged the pilot on again, and the Chinook's vast shadow fell again over the upturned faces of people transformed, by this telling, into comic gibbering stickmen just waiting to be blown away like the toothpick houses they lived in. As I brought the helicopter down on them I looked over at Jan and saw her watching me with an expression

so thoroughly disappointed as to be devoid of reproach. I
didn't like it. I felt the worst kind of anger, the anger that
proceeds from shame. So instead of easing up I laid it on
even thicker, playing the whole thing for laughs, as cruel
as I could make them, because after all Dicky had been
there, and what more than that could I ever hope to have
in common with her?

When I got to the end Dicky banged his forehead on the
table to indicate maximum mirth. Sleepy leaned back with
a startled expression and gave me the once-over. "Hey," he
said, "great shirt, I used to have one just like it."

I called Vera the next morning from a pancake house, my
pockets sagging with quarters. It was the first time I'd heard
her voice in over a year, and the sound of it made everything
in between seem vaporous, unreal. We began to talk as if
resuming a conversation from the night before, teasing,
implying, setting each other off. We talked like lovers. I
found myself shaking, I was so maddened not to be able to
see her.

When I hung up, the panic of loneliness I'd come awake
to that morning was even worse. It made no sense to me
that Vera was there and I was here. The others too – my
mother, my friends, Geoffrey and Priscilla. They had a baby
now, my nephew Nicholas, born while I was in Vietnam. I
still hadn't laid eyes on him.

I made up my mind to fly home the next day.

That last night, the old man and I went out to dinner.
For a change of pace we drove down to Redondo Beach,
to a stylish French restaurant where, it turned out, they
required a coat and tie. Neither of us had a tie so they

supplied us with a pair of identical clip-ons, mile-wide Carnaby Street foulards with gigantic red polka dots. We looked like clowns. My father had never in his life insulted his person with such a costume and it took him a while to submit to it, but he came around. We had a good time, quietly, neither of us drinking much. Over coffee I told him I was leaving.

He rolled with it, said he'd figured it was about time I checked in with my mother. Then he asked when I'd be coming back.

"I'm not sure," I said.

"If you're thinking of going to school here, you'll want to give yourself plenty of time to look around, find some digs."

"Dad, I have to say, I've been giving that a lot of thought."

He waited. Then he said, "So you won't be going to school here."

"No. I'm sorry."

He waved away the apology. "All for the b-best, chum. My view exactly. You should aim higher." He looked at me in the kindest way. He had beautiful eyes, the old man, and they had remained beautiful while his face had gone to ruin all around them. He reached over and squeezed my arm. "You'll be back."

"Definitely. That's a promise."

"They all come back for Doctor Wolff's famous rest cure."

"I was thinking maybe next summer. As soon as I get myself really going on something."

"Of course," he said. "Filial duty. Have to look in on

your old pop, make sure he's keeping his nose clean." He tried to smile but couldn't, his very flesh failed him, and that was the closest I came to changing my mind. I meant it when I said I'd be back but it sounded like a bald-faced lie, as if the truth was already known to both of us that I would not be back and that he would live alone and die alone, as he did, two years later, and that this was what was meant by my leaving. Still, after the first doubt I felt no doubt at all. Even that brief hesitation began to seem like mawkish shamming.

He was staring at my wrist. "Let's have a look at that watch."

I handed it over, a twenty-dollar Seiko that ran well and looked like it cost every penny. My father took off his Heuer chronograph and pushed it across the table. It was a thing of beauty. I didn't hold back for a second. I picked it up, hefted it, and strapped it on.

"Made for you," he said. "Now let's get these g-goddamned ties off."

Geoffrey noticed the chronograph a few nights after I got home. We were on his living room floor, drinking and playing cards. He admired the watch and asked how much it set me back. If I'd had my wits about me I would have lied to him, but I didn't. I said the old man had given it to me. "The old man gave it to you?" His face clouded over and I thought, Ah, nuts. I didn't know for sure what Geoffrey was thinking, but I was thinking about all those checks he'd sent out to Manhattan Beach. "I doubt if he paid for it," I said. Geoffrey didn't answer for a while. Then he said, "Probably not," and picked up his cards.

●　　●　　●

Vera's family owned a big spread in Maryland. After a round of homecoming visits, I left Washington and moved down there with her to help with the haying and see if we couldn't compose ourselves and find a way to live together. We did not. In the past she'd counted on me to control my moods so that she could give free rein to her own and still have a ticket back. Now I was as touchy and ungoverned as Vera, and often worse. She began to let her bassett hound eat at the table with her, in a chair, at his own place setting, because, she said, she had to have some decent company.

We were such bad medicine together that her mother, the most forbearing of souls, went back to Washington to get away from us. That left us alone in the house, an old plantation manor. Vera's family didn't have the money to keep it up, and the air of the place was moldy and regretful, redolent of better days. Portraits of Vera's planter ancestors hung from every wall. I had the feeling they were watching me with detestation and scorn, as if I were a usurping cad, a dancing master with oily hair and scented fingers.

While the sun was high we worked outside. In the afternoons I went upstairs to the servants' wing, now empty, where I'd set up an office. I had begun another novel. I knew it wasn't very good, but I also knew that it was the best I could do just then and that I had to keep doing it if I ever wanted to get any better. These words would never be read by anyone, I understood, but even in sinking out of sight they made the ground more solid under my hope to write well.

Not that I didn't like what I was writing as I filled up the pages. Only at the end of the day, reading over what I'd done, working through it with a green pencil, did I see how far I was from where I wanted to be. In the very act of writing I felt pleased with what I did. There was the pleasure of having words come to me, and the pleasure of ordering them, re-ordering them, weighing one against another. Pleasure also in the imagination of the story, the feeling that it could mean something. Mostly I was glad to find out that I could write at all. In writing you work toward a result you won't see for years, and can't be sure you'll ever see. It takes stamina and self-mastery and faith. It demands those things of you, then gives them back with a little extra, a surprise to keep you coming. It toughens you and clears your head. I could feel it happening. I was saving my life with every word I wrote, and I knew it.

In the servants' quarters I was a man of reason. In the rest of the house, something else. For two months Vera and I tied knots in each other's nerves, trying to make love happen again, knowing it wouldn't. The sadness of what we were doing finally became intolerable, and I left for Washington. When I called to say my last good-bye she asked me to wait, then picked up the phone again and told me she had a pistol in her hand and would shoot herself if I didn't promise to come back that same night.

"Vera, really, you already pulled this."

"When?"

"Before we got engaged."

"That was you? I thought it was Leland." She started to laugh. Then she stopped. "That doesn't mean I won't do it. Toby? I'm serious."

"Bang," I said, and hung up.

A week later I traveled to England with friends. When they

returned home I stayed on, first in London, then in Oxford, reading, hitting the pubs, walking the countryside. It was restful: the greenness, the fetishized civility, the quaint, exquisite class consciousness I could observe without despair because as a Yank I had no place in it. My money stretched double and nobody talked about Vietnam. Every afternoon I went back to my room and wrote. I saw little to complain of in this life except that it couldn't go on. I knew I had to make a move, somehow buy into the world outside my window.

Some people I'd met encouraged me to take the Oxford entrance exams in early December. That left four and a half months to prepare myself in Latin, French, English history and literature. I knew I couldn't do it alone, so I hired university tutors in each of the test areas. After they'd made it clear how irregular this project was, how unlikely, they warmed to it. They took it on in the spirit of a great game, strategizing like underdog coaches, devising shortcuts, second-guessing the examiners, working me into the ground. After the first few weeks my Latin tutor, Miss Knight, demanded that I take a room in her house so she could crack the whip even harder. Miss Knight wore men's clothing and ran an animal hospital out of her kitchen. When she worked in the garden birds flew down and perched on her shoulder. She very much preferred Greek to English, and Latin to Greek, and said things like, "I can't *wait* to set you loose on Virgil!" She cooked my meals so I wouldn't lose time and drilled me on vocabulary and grammar as I ate. She kept in touch with my other tutors and proofread my essays for them, scratching furiously at the pompous locutions with which

I tried to conceal my ignorance and uncertainty. All those months she fed her life straight into mine, and because of her I passed the examination and was matriculated into the university to read for an honors degree in English Language and Literature.

Oxford: for four years it was my school and my home. I made lifelong friends there, traveled, fell in love, did well in my studies. Yet I seldom speak of it, because to say "When I was at Oxford . . ." sounds suspect even to me, like the opening of one of my father's bullshit stories. Even at the time I was never quite convinced of the reality of my presence there. Day after day, walking those narrow lanes and lush courtyards, looking up to see a slip of cloud drifting behind a spire, I had to stop in disbelief. I couldn't get used to it, but that was all right. After every catch of irreality I felt an acute consciousness of good luck; it forced me to recognize where I was, and give thanks. This practice had a calming effect that served me well. I'd carried a little bit of Vietnam home with me in the form of something like malaria that wasn't malaria, ulcers, colitis, insomnia, and persistent terrors when I did sleep. Coming up shaky after a bad night, I could do wonders for myself simply by looking out the window.

It was the best the world had to give, and yet the very richness of the offering made me restless in the end. Comfort turned against itself. More and more I had the sense of avoiding some necessary difficulty, of growing in cleverness and facility without growing otherwise. Of being once again adrift.

I was in the Bodleian Library one night, doing a translation from the West Saxon Gospels for my Old

English class. The assigned passage was from the Sermon on the Mount. It came hard, every line sending me back to the grammar or the glossary, until the last six verses, which gave themselves up all at once, blooming in my head in the same words I'd heard as a boy, shouted from evangelical pulpits and the stages of revival meetings. They told the story of the wise man who built his house upon a rock and the foolish man who built his house upon the sand. "And the rain descended, and the floods came, and the winds blew, and beat upon that house; and it fell; and great was the fall of it."

I'd forgotten I'd ever known these words. When they spoke themselves to me that night I was surprised, and overcome by a feeling of strangeness to myself and everything around me. I looked up from the table. From where I sat I could see the lights of my college, Hertford, where Jonathan Swift and Evelyn Waugh had once been students. I was in a country far from my own, and even farther from the kind of life I'd once seemed destined for. If you'd asked me how I got here I couldn't have told you. The winds that had blown me here could have blown me anywhere, even from the face of the earth. It was unaccountable. But I *was* here, in this moment, which all the other moments of my life had conspired to bring me to. And with this moment came these words, served on me like a writ. I copied out my translation in plain English, and thought that, yes, I would do well to build my house upon a rock, whatever that meant.

Last Shot

George Orwell wrote an essay called "How the Poor Die" about his experience in the public ward of a Paris hospital during his lean years. I happened to read it not long ago because one of my sons was writing a paper on Orwell, and I wanted to be able to talk with him about it. The essay was new to me. I liked it for its gallows humor and cool watchfulness. Orwell had me in the palm of his hand until I came to this line: "It is a great thing to die in your own bed, though it is better still to die in your boots."

It stopped me cold. Figure of speech or not, he meant it, and anyway the words could not be separated from their martial beat and the rhetoric that promotes dying young as some kind of good deal. They affected me like an insult. I was so angry I had to get up and walk it off. Later I looked up the date of the essay and found that Orwell had written it before Spain and World War II, before he'd had the chance to see what dying in your boots actually means. (The truth is, many of those who "die in their boots" are literally blown right out of them.)

Several men I knew were killed in Vietnam. Most of them I didn't know well, and haven't thought much about since. But my friend Hugh Pierce was a different case. We were very close, and would have gone on being close, as I am with my other good friends from those years. He would have been one of them, another godfather for my children, another bighearted man for them to admire and stay up late listening to. An old friend, someone I couldn't fool, who would hold me to the best dreams of my youth as I would hold him to his.

Instead of remembering Hugh as I knew him, I too often think of him in terms of what he never had a chance to be. The things the rest of us know, he will not know. He will not know what it is to make a life with someone else. To have a child slip in beside him as he lies reading on a Sunday morning. To work at, and then look back on, a labor of years. Watch the decline of his parents, and attend their dissolution. Lose faith. Pray anyway. Persist. We are made to persist, to complete the whole tour. That's how we find out who we are.

I know it's wrong to think of Hugh as an absence, a thwarted shadow. It's my awareness of his absence that I'm describing, and maybe something else, some embarrassment, kept hidden even from myself, that I went on without him. To think of Hugh like this is to make selfish use of him. So, of course, is making him a character in a book. Let me at least remember him as he was.

He loved to jump. He was the one who started the "My Girl" business, singing and doing the Stroll to the door of the plane. I always take the position behind him, hand on his back, according to the drill we've been taught. I do not love to jump, to tell the truth, but I feel better about it when I'm connected to Hugh. Men are disappearing out the door ahead of us, the sound of the engine is getting louder. Hugh is singing in falsetto, doing a goofy routine with his hands. Just before he reaches the door he looks back and says something to me. I can't hear him for the wind. What? I say. He yells, *Are we having fun?* He laughs at the look on my face, then turns and takes his place in the door, and jumps, and is gone.